Dear Friend,

I am pleased to send you this copy of *40 Lives in 40 Days* by my friend John MacArthur, pastor of Grace Community Church, bestselling author, and founder of the international broadcast program *Grace to You*. Dr. MacArthur has also led seminars at the Billy Graham Training Center at The Cove.

Throughout this book, you'll explore 40 Biblical lives—from Old Testament women to Christ's beloved disciples. Each chapter includes a short biography along with questions that allow you to discover how God moved in each person's life—for His purposes and His glory. It's my prayer that this resource will inspire and encourage you to "*walk in a manner worthy of the calling to which you have been called*" (Ephesians 4:1, ESV).

For more than 70 years, God has used the Billy Graham Evangelistic Association and friends like you to reach people all over the world with the Gospel. I'm so thankful for the ways He has worked—and what He will do in the years ahead.

If you represent one of the lives the Lord has touched, we would love to hear from you. Your story has the power to impact the lives of so many others. May God richly bless you.

Sincerely,

Franklin Graham
President

If you would like to know more about our ministry, please contact us:

IN THE U.S.:
Billy Graham Evangelistic Association
1 Billy Graham Parkway
Charlotte, NC 28201-0001
BillyGraham.org
info@bgea.org
Toll-free: 1-877-247-2426

IN CANADA:
Billy Graham Evangelistic
    Association of Canada
20 Hopewell Way NE
Calgary, AB T3J 5H5
BillyGraham.ca
Toll-free: 1-888-393-0003

40 LIVES IN 40 DAYS

Experiencing God's Grace Through the Bible's Most Compelling Characters

JOHN MACARTHUR

THOMAS NELSON®
Since 1798

40 Lives in 40 Days

© 2022 John MacArthur

Portions of this book were excerpted and adapted from: *Twelve Ordinary Men*, *Twelve Extraordinary Women*, *Unlikely Heroes*, *A Tale of Two Sons*, *The Gospel According to Paul*, and *The Gospel According to Jesus*.

Published in Nashville, Tennessee, by Thomas Nelson. Thomas Nelson is a registered trademark of HarperCollins Christian Publishing, Inc.

Thomas Nelson titles may be purchased in bulk for educational, business, fundraising, or sales promotional use. For information, please email SpecialMarkets@ThomasNelson.com.

Unless otherwise noted, Scripture quotations marked NKJV are taken from the New King James Version®. Copyright © 1982 by Thomas Nelson. Used by permission. All rights reserved.

Scripture quotations marked ESV are taken from the ESV® Bible (The Holy Bible, English Standard Version®). Copyright © 2001 by Crossway, a publishing ministry of Good News Publishers. Used by permission. All rights reserved.

Scripture quotations marked NASB are taken from the New American Standard Bible® (NASB). Copyright © 1960, 1962, 1963, 1968, 1971, 1972, 1973, 1975, 1977, 1995 by The Lockman Foundation. Used by permission. www.lockman.org

ISBN 978-0-7852-9561-7 (audiobook)
ISBN 978-0-7852-9560-0 (eBook)
ISBN 978-1-4041-1948-2 (Custom)

Library of Congress Cataloging-in-Publication Data on File

ISBN 978-0-7852-9559-4

Printed in the United States of America

23 24 25 26 27 LBC 5 4 3 2 1

Contents

Simon Peter

*"Simon, son of Jonah, do you love Me
more than these? . . . Feed my lambs."*

JOHN 21:15

With the long nights required to bring in a decent haul
and the violent storms that could erupt with barely
a moment's notice, being a fisherman on the Sea of
Galilee was a rough job. In fact, "rough" is how one
might describe Simon before he was forever changed by
Jesus. Simon, the fisherman-turned-disciple, was impetuous, impulsive, and overeager. He often put his foot in
his mouth, and he has the notable distinction of being
the only person in the Gospels Jesus addressed as Satan.
And yet, despite Simon's turbulent persona, Jesus gave
him the nickname *Peter,* or *Rock.*

In every list of disciples found in the New Testament, Peter is listed first. He was part of Jesus' inner circle, and it seems he enjoyed a special relationship with the Lord. Simon could certainly be rough around the edges, but that didn't prevent Jesus from utilizing His friend for kingdom leadership. By nature Simon was brash, vacillating, and undependable. He tended to make great promises he couldn't follow through with. He was one of those people who lunges wholeheartedly into something but then bails out before finishing. Jesus changed Simon's name, it appears, because He wanted the nickname to be a perpetual reminder to him about who he *should* be.

> Jesus chose Simon Peter not because he was doing everything right but because He knew his great potential.

Peter was exactly like most Christians—both carnal and spiritual. He succumbed to the habits of the flesh sometimes; he functioned in the Spirit other times. He was sinful sometimes, but other times he acted the way a righteous man ought to act. This vacillating man—sometimes Simon, sometimes Peter—was the leader of the Twelve.

Jesus chose Simon Peter not because he was

doing everything right but because He knew his great potential. Even though he needed training and life experience, Peter had the raw materials that make an excellent leader.

First, he was highly inquisitive. It was usually Peter who asked the Lord to explain His difficult sayings (Matthew 15:15; Luke 12:41). It was Peter who asked how often he needed to forgive (Matthew 18:21). It was Peter who asked about the withered fig tree (Mark 11:21). He always wanted to know more, to understand better.

Second, Simon Peter was willing to take the initiative. When Jesus asked His disciples, "But who do you say that I am?" it was Peter who answered boldly (and correctly): "You are the Christ, the Son of the living God." This willingness to take the initiative sometimes ended badly, however—like in the garden of Gethsemane when Peter, staring down hundreds of armed soldiers, swung his sword at one of the high priest's servants and cut off his ear.

Finally, Peter was the sort of person who always wanted to be personally involved. It was he who asked Jesus if he could get out of the boat and join Him in walking on the water. It was also Peter who followed Jesus after He was arrested. And in the courtyard of the high priest's house, Peter was close enough that Jesus could turn and look him in the eyes (Luke 22:61).

Of course, the reason Jesus turned to look at Simon Peter was that he had just denied knowing the Lord three times. Though the fisherman had done something terrible, Jesus was not done with him; He still planned to make him into the Rock He knew Peter could be. He knew Peter would deny Him; He had predicted it and had even given Satan permission to sift his friend (Luke 22:31). But Jesus told Simon Peter, "I have prayed for you, that your faith should not fail; and when you have returned to Me, strengthen your brethren" (v. 32).

What was this all about? People with natural leadership abilities often tend to be short on compassion, lousy comforters, and impatient with others. They don't stop very long to care for the wounded as they pursue their goals. Simon Peter needed to learn compassion through his own ordeal, so that when it was over, he could strengthen his brothers and sisters in theirs. Jesus took the rough fisherman Simon Peter, full of inquisitiveness, initiative, and a need to be personally involved, and cultivated within him a spirit of submission, restraint, humility, and love—all to make him live up to his nickname, Peter, the Rock.

Thankfully, Jesus doesn't leave us to smooth out our rough edges on our own. He calls us to be transformed in Him into the people He intends us to be.

What should we make of the name Jesus chose for Peter?

_____

_____

_____

What do we learn from the fact that Jesus did not reject Peter despite his brashness?

_____

_____

_____

Which of his characteristics contributed to making Peter a good leader? How are you cultivating those traits in your own life?

_____

_____

_____

Andrew

He first found his own brother Simon,
and said to him, "We have found the
Messiah."

JOHN 1:41

Unlike his brother Simon Peter, who tended to be impetuous, to rush ahead foolishly, and to say the wrong thing at the wrong time, Andrew was quiet, reserved, and always seemed to know the right thing to say. Whenever he acted apart from the other disciples, he did what was right. In fact, almost everything the Bible tells us about Andrew shows that he had the right heart for effective ministry in the background. He did not seek to be the center of attention, nor did he seem to resent those who labored in the limelight. He was evidently pleased to do what he could with the gifts and calling God had bestowed on him, and he allowed the others to do likewise.

Andrew first met the Lord while he was a disciple of John the Baptist. Andrew was standing next to John the Baptist on the banks of the Jordan River when Jesus walked by and John said, "Behold the Lamb of God!" (John 1:35–36). Andrew immediately left John's side and began to follow Jesus (v. 37). Don't imagine he was being fickle or untrue to their mentor. Quite the opposite. John the Baptist had already said in the most plain and forthright terms that he was only the forerunner of the Messiah. He had come to prepare the way and to point people in the right direction. That is why as soon as Andrew heard John the Baptist identify Jesus as the Lamb of God, he instantly, eagerly left John to follow Christ.

Almost as soon as Andrew became a disciple of Jesus, he also became an evangelist: "He first found his own brother Simon, and said to him, 'We have found the Messiah' (which is translated, the Christ). And he brought him to Jesus" (vv. 41–42). The news was too good to keep to himself, so Andrew went and found the one person in the world whom he most loved—whom he most wanted to know Jesus—and he led him to Christ. Andrew would have been fully aware of Simon Peter's tendency to domineer. He must have known full well that as soon as Peter entered the company of disciples, he would take charge and Andrew would be relegated to a secondary status. Yet Andrew brought his older brother anyway. That fact alone says much about his character.

But that wasn't the only time Andrew brought someone to meet the Messiah. On one occasion, Jesus had gone to a mountain to try to be alone with His disciples. As often happened when He took a break from public ministry, the clamoring multitudes tracked Him down. It was nearing time to eat, and bread would be the object lesson in the message Jesus would preach to the multitude. So He made it clear that He wanted to feed the multitude. But where would they get bread to feed more than five thousand people? Philip calculated that even two hundred denarii would not be enough to

Andrew's legacy is the example he left to show us that it's often the little things that count— the individual people, the insignificant gifts, and the inconspicuous service.

buy food for the multitude. Now, a denarius was a day's pay for a common laborer, so two hundred denarii would be approximately eight months' wages—no small sum.

It seemed an impossible problem, but that didn't stop Andrew from speaking up: "There is a lad here who has five barley loaves and two small fish" (John 6:9). Of course, even Andrew knew that five barley loaves and two small fish would not be enough to feed five thousand people, but (in his typical fashion) he brought the boy to Jesus anyway. Something in him seemed to understand that no gift is insignificant in the hands of Jesus.

Some people won't play in the band unless they can hit the big drum. James and John had that tendency. So did Peter. But not Andrew. He was more concerned about bringing people to Jesus than about who got the credit or who was in charge. Andrew is the very picture of all those who labor quietly in humble places, "not with eyeservice, as men-pleasers, but as bondservants of Christ, doing the will of God from the heart" (Ephesians 6:6).

Andrew's legacy is the example he left to show us that it's often the little things that count—the individual people, the insignificant gifts, and the inconspicuous service. Thank God for people like Andrew. They're

the quiet individuals, laboring faithfully but inconspic-
uously, giving seemingly insignificant yet sacrificial gifts,
who accomplish the most for the Lord.

Which single trait best characterizes Andrew?

_____

_____

_____

*What does Andrew's first instinct, upon coming
to Christ, tell us about his priorities? How do you
reflect the same priorities in your own life?*

_____

_____

_____

*Do you judge your service to the Lord with the
same judgment Andrew used? Why or why not?
Choose a few specific areas in which you could
adjust your thinking.*

_____

_____

_____

James

*Now about that time Herod the king
stretched out his hand to harass some
from the church. Then he killed James
the brother of John with the sword.*

ACTS 12:1-2

Of Jesus' twelve disciples, three were part of His inner circle—Peter, James, and John. These three were the only ones Jesus permitted to go with Him when He raised Jairus's daughter from the dead (Mark 5:37). The same group witnessed Jesus' glory on the Mount of Transfiguration (Matthew 17:1). And these were the three the Lord urged to pray with Him privately in Gethsemane (Mark 14:33). From this intimate group of three disciples, the one the Gospels tell us the least about is James.

But even with the few details about the apostle James given to us in Scripture, what we do have is a portrait of a man with tremendous zeal for the Lord. This passion sometimes manifested in ways that were misguided and arrogant, but if I have to choose between a man of burning, flaming, enthusiasm with a potential for failure on the one hand, and a cold compromiser on the other hand, I'll take the man with passion every time.

Just as Jesus gave the name *Peter* to Simon Peter, He also gave a new name to James and John. Probably owing to their reckless tendencies, they were dubbed *Boanerges*, or "Sons of Thunder" (Mark 3:17). We get our best glimpse of why James and John were known as the Sons of Thunder in Luke 9:51–56. Jesus was preparing to pass through Samaria on His way to Jerusalem for the Passover. Since the party traveling with Jesus was fairly large, He sent messengers ahead to arrange accommodations. Being a devout Jew on His way to worship in Jerusalem, Jesus represented everything the Samaritans despised. So they summarily rejected the request for lodging. The problem was not that there was no room for them in the inn; the problem was that the Samaritans were being deliberately inhospitable. James and John, the Sons of Thunder, were instantly filled with passionate outrage. They said, "Lord, do You want us to command fire to come down from heaven and consume them, just as Elijah did?" (Luke 9:54; see also 2 Kings 1).

After all this time with Jesus, how could the brothers have missed the spirit of so much He had taught? He was on a mission of rescue, not judgment. "For God did not send His Son into the world to condemn the world, but that the world through Him might be saved" (John 3:17). Even so, it is far better to get fired up with righteous wrath than to sit passively and endure insults against Christ. So their resentment over seeing Christ deliberately slighted is admirable in some measure, even though their reaction was tainted with arrogance and their proposed remedy to the problem completely out of line.

We get another insight into James's character in Mark 10:35–45. Here we discover that James was not only fervent, passionate, zealous, and insensitive; he was also ambitious and overconfident. And in this case, he and his brother John engaged in a furtive attempt to gain status over the other apostles:

Then James and John, the sons of Zebedee, came to Him, saying, "Teacher, we want You to do for us whatever we ask."

> And He said to them, "What do you want Me to do for you?"
>
> They said to Him, "Grant us that we may sit, one on Your right hand and the other on Your left, in Your glory." (Mark 10:35–37)

Jesus' reply subtly reminded them that suffering is the prelude to glory: "Are you able to drink the cup that I drink, and be baptized with the baptism that I am baptized with?" (v. 38). James wanted a crown of glory; Jesus gave him a cup of suffering. He wanted power; Jesus gave him servanthood. He wanted a place of prominence; Jesus gave him a martyr's grave. He wanted to rule; Jesus gave him a sword—not to wield but to be the instrument of his own execution. Fourteen years after this, James would become the first of the Twelve to be killed for his faith (Acts 12:2).

> It is far better to get fired up with righteous wrath than to sit passively and endure insults against Christ.

Clearly, James never stopped being zealous for Christ. He was a true Son of Thunder until the end. Such passion must always be harnessed and tempered

with love. But if it is surrendered to the control of the
Holy Spirit and blended with patience and longsuffering,
it can be a marvelous instrument in the hands of God.
The life of James offers clear proof of that.

Explain the nickname Jesus gave James and John.

_____

_____

_____

*What was right in James and John's suggestion
regarding the Samaritans? What was wrong?*

_____

_____

_____

*What does James's martyrdom tell us about his
character? How should and shouldn't you emulate
what you see there?*

_____

_____

_____

John

*My little children, let us not love in
word or in tongue, but in deed and in
truth.*

1 JOHN 3:18

When we think of the apostle John today, we usually
think of a tenderhearted, elderly apostle. As the elder
statesman of the church near the end of the first century,
he was universally beloved and respected for his devotion to Christ and his great love for the saints worldwide.
That is precisely why he earned the epithet "the apostle
of love."

As a young man, however, John was not unlike his
older brother, James. They were cut from the same cloth.
John was volatile, brash, and aggressive. Moreover, he

was passionate, zealous, and personally ambitious. But John aged well. Under the control of the Holy Spirit, all his liabilities were exchanged for assets. Compare the young disciple with the aged patriarch, and you'll see that as he matured, his areas of greatest weakness all developed into his greatest strengths. He's an amazing example of what should happen to us as we grow in Christ—allowing the Lord's strength to be made perfect in our weakness.

Much of what we know about John comes from his own writings. The way John wrote was a reflection of his personality. Truth was his passion, and he seemed to bend over backward not to make it fuzzy. He spoke in black-and-white, absolute, certain terms, and he did not waste ink coloring in all the gray areas. He gave rules of thumb without listing all the exceptions. Jesus Himself often spoke in absolutes just like that, and John no doubt learned his teaching style from the Lord. Although John always wrote with a warm, personal, pastoral tone, what he wrote does not always make for soothing reading. It does, however, always reflect his deep convictions and his absolute devotion to the truth.

Clearly, there is nothing inherently wrong with zeal for the truth, a desire to succeed, or a sense of confidence.

Those are all legitimate virtues. But even a virtue out of balance can become an impediment to spiritual health—just as truth out of balance can lead to serious error. A person out of balance is unsteady. Imbalance in one's personal character is a form of intemperance—a lack of self-control—and that is a sin in and of itself. So it is a very dangerous thing to push any point of truth or any character quality to an undue extreme.

That is what we see in the life of the younger disciple John. On one occasion, John told Jesus, "Teacher, we saw someone who does not follow us casting out demons in Your name, and we forbade him because he does not follow us" (Mark 9:38). This was sectarianism—rebuking a man for ministering in Jesus' name just because he didn't belong to the group. This shows the intolerance of John, a Son of Thunder. This was the narrowness, the ambition, the desire to have the status all for himself and not share it with anybody else—all of which too often characterized John in his younger years.

> John is an amazing example of what should happen to us as we grow in Christ—allowing the Lord's strength to be made perfect in our weakness.

But three years with Jesus began to transform a self-centered fanatic into a mature man of balance. Three years with Jesus moved this Son of Thunder toward becoming an apostle of love. At the very points where he was most imbalanced, Christ gave him equilibrium, and in the process John was transformed from a bigoted hothead into a loving, godly elder statesman for the early church.

John was always committed to truth, and there's certainly nothing wrong with that, but it is not enough. Zeal for the truth must be balanced by love for people. Truth without love has no decency; it's just brutality. On the other hand, love without truth has no character; it's just hypocrisy.

Many people are just as imbalanced as John was, only in the other direction. They place too much emphasis on the love side of the fulcrum. They talk a lot about love and tolerance, but they utterly lack any concern for the truth. On the other hand, there are many who have all their theological ducks in a row and know their doctrine but are unloving and self-exalting. Their lack of love cripples the power of the truth they profess to revere.

The truly godly person must cultivate both virtues in equal proportions. If you could wish for anything in your sanctification, wish for that. If you pursue anything in the spiritual realm, pursue a perfect balance of truth and love. Know the truth, and uphold it in love.

What made the difference in John's character from his youth to his old age? How are you seeing the same maturation process in your own life?

_____

_____

_____

What did John devote his life to? How do you manifest sharing the same passion?

_____

_____

_____

Explain the nature of intemperance and imbalance—and their dangers. In what areas of your own life do you see this tendency?

_____

_____

_____

Philip

Philip answered Him, "Two hundred denarii worth of bread is not sufficient for them, that every one of them may have a little."

JOHN 6:7

While Andrew, John, Peter, and, presumably, James all found Jesus either directly or indirectly through the ministry of John the Baptist, Philip has the distinction of being the first disciple whom Jesus sought out. John writes, "The following day Jesus wanted to go to Galilee, and He found Philip and said to him, 'Follow Me'" (John 1:43). Apparently, Philip was also in the wilderness with John the Baptist, and before returning to Galilee, Jesus pursued him and invited Philip to join the other disciples.

It is obvious that Philip already had a seeking heart. The evidence for this can be seen in how he responded to Jesus. "Philip found Nathanael and said to him, 'We have found Him of whom Moses in the law, and also the prophets, wrote; Jesus of Nazareth, the son of Joseph'" (John 1:45). Of course, a seeking heart is always evidence that God is sovereignly drawing the person, for as Jesus said, "No one can come to Me unless the Father who sent Me draws him" (John 6:44).

Philip and Nathanael, like the first four disciples, had been studying the Law and the Prophets, and were seeking the Messiah. That is why they had all gone to the wilderness to hear John the Baptist in the first place. So when Jesus came to Philip and said, "Follow Me," his ears, his eyes, and his heart were already open, and he was prepared to follow.

> A seeking heart is always evidence that God is sovereignly drawing the person.

Philip was ready. He was expectant. His heart was prepared. And he received Jesus gladly, unhesitatingly, as Messiah. No reluctance. No disbelief. He knew instantly that he had come to the end of his search. That is frankly out of character for Philip, and it reveals to what a great degree the Lord had prepared his heart. His natural tendency might have been to hold back, doubt, ask questions, and wait and see. He was not usually a very decisive person. But thankfully, in this case, he was already being drawn to Christ by the Father. And as Jesus said, "All that the Father gives Me *will* come to Me" (John 6:37, emphasis added).

Philip's natural inclinations were on full display just before Jesus fed the five thousand. John 6:5 reads, "Then Jesus lifted up His eyes, and seeing a great multitude coming toward Him, He said to Philip, 'Where shall we buy bread, that these may eat?'" Why did He single out Philip and ask him? John tells us: "This He said to test him, for He Himself knew what He would do" (v. 6). Philip was apparently the apostolic administrator—the bean counter. Whether officially or unofficially, he seems to have been the one who was always concerned with organization and protocol. He was the type of person who in every meeting says, "I don't think we can do that"—the master of the impossible. And apparently, as far as he was concerned, almost everything fit into that category.

Philip already had his calculations prepared: "Philip answered Him, 'Two hundred denarii worth of bread is not sufficient for them, that every one of them may have a little'" (John 6:7). He had apparently been thinking through the difficulties of the food supply from the moment he first saw the crowd. Instead of thinking, *What a glorious occasion! Jesus is going to teach this crowd. What a tremendous opportunity for the Lord!*—all pessimistic Philip could see was the impossibility of the situation. As a result, he lost the opportunity to see the reward of faith.

As Jesus taught His disciples elsewhere, "If you have faith as a mustard seed, you will say to this mountain, 'Move from here to there,' and it will move; and nothing will be impossible for you" (Matthew 17:20). Philip needed to learn that lesson. Everything seemed impossible to him. He needed to set aside his materialistic, pragmatic, commonsense concerns and learn to lay hold of the supernatural potential of faith.

Philip was a man of limited ability, weak faith, and imperfect understanding. He could be skeptical, analytical, pessimistic, reluctant, and unsure. He was slow to understand, slow to trust, and slow to see beyond the immediate circumstances. If we were interviewing Philip for the role to which Jesus called him, we might say, "He's out." But Jesus said, "He's exactly what I'm looking for. My strength is made perfect in weakness."

Thankfully, the Lord still uses people just like Philip today—lots of them.

Name the many ways, even in this short profile, we see Christ showing grace to Philip. How do you see Him doing the same in your own life?

_____

_____

_____

How do we see Philip's greatest strengths being also his greatest liabilities? How successful are you at frankly assessing yourself along the same lines?

_____

_____

_____

What was Philip's greatest need? Why was this deficiency no barrier to Christ's choosing him?

_____

_____

_____

Nathanael

Jesus saw Nathanael coming toward Him and said of him, "Behold, an Israelite indeed, in whom is no deceit!"

JOHN 1:47

"Can anything good come out of Nazareth?" (John 1:46). That was Nathanael's response to the news that his good friend Philip had met the Messiah.

It was inconceivable to Nathanael that the Christ would come out of a place like Nazareth. It was an uncultured town, full of evil, corrupt, and populated with sinful people. Nathanael simply did not anticipate that anything good could come from there. And he was oblivious to the rather obvious fact that he himself had come from an equally contemptible community,

Cana. Though Nathanael's question to Philip revealed his prejudice, it also revealed something else. As Jesus Himself put it, "Behold, an Israelite indeed, in whom is no deceit!" (v. 47).

Can you imagine a more wonderful thing than to have words of personal commendation like that come out of the mouth of Jesus? It would be one thing to hear that at the end of your life. We often hear eulogies at funerals that extol the virtues of the deceased. But how would you like Jesus to say that about you from the very start?

> Nathanael's love for God and his desire to see the Messiah were genuine.

This speaks volumes about Nathanael's character. He was purehearted from the beginning. Certainly, he was human. He had sinful faults. His mind was tainted by a degree of prejudice. But his heart was not poisoned by deceit. He was no hypocrite. His love for God and his desire to see the Messiah were genuine. His heart was sincere and without guile. Jesus refers to him as "an Israelite indeed." The word in the Greek text is *alēthōs*, meaning "truly, genuinely." He was an authentic Israelite.

This is not a reference to his physical descent from

Abraham. Jesus was not talking about genetics. He was linking Nathanael's status as a true Israelite to the fact that he was without deceit. His guilelessness is what defined him as a true Israelite. For the most part, the Israelites of Jesus' day were not real, because they were hypocrites. They were phonies. They lived life with a veneer of spirituality, but they were not genuine spiritual children of Abraham. Nathanael, however, was the real thing. His devotion to God was real. He was a truly righteous man—flawed by sin as we all are—but justified before God through a true and living faith.

Astonished that Jesus seemed to have pegged him as a person who was honest to a fault, Nathanael asked, "How do you know me?" He might have meant, "Are You just flattering me? How could You possibly know what is in my heart?"

Jesus answered, "Before Philip called you, when you were under the fig tree, I saw you" (v. 48). This put a whole different spin on things. This was not flattery; it was omniscience! Jesus wasn't physically present to see Nathanael under the fig tree; Nathanael knew that. Suddenly, he realized he was standing in the presence of Someone who could see into his very heart with an omniscient eye.

Nathanael proclaimed, "You are the Son of God! You are the King of Israel!" (v. 49). He knew the Old Testament. He was familiar with what the prophets had said. He knew whom to look for. And now, regardless of the fact that Jesus came from Nazareth, His omniscience, His spiritual insight, and His ability to read his heart were enough to convince Nathanael that Jesus was indeed the true Messiah.

Jesus affirmed Nathanael's faith and promised him that he would see even greater things: "Most assuredly, I say to you, hereafter you shall see heaven open, and the angels of God ascending and descending upon the Son of Man" (v. 51; see also Genesis 28:12). Jesus is the ladder that connects heaven and earth. During the next three years, Nathanael would see an unfolding panorama of spiritual reality.

Scripture doesn't tell us much about Nathanael. But we do know he was a true disciple from the start. Most of Jesus' disciples struggled just to come to the place where Nathanael stood after his first meeting with Christ. The ministry of Christ only affirmed what he already knew to be true. How wonderful to see someone so trustworthy and trusting from the very beginning!

As Nathanael's testimony shows us, hypocrisy has no

place in the life of a Christian. Jesus calls us to be genuine and without guile. And though we may have our own prejudices and blind spots to work on, Jesus can still use us for His glory.

How did Christ summarize Nathanael's character? Could He say the same of you? Why or why not?

_____

_____

_____

What made Nathanael a true Israelite?

_____

_____

_____

Consider both Nathanael's hypocritical prejudice and his guilelessness. What did Christ do with both? How does that relate to the basis on which Nathanael was justified as truly righteous?

_____

_____

_____

Matthew

*He saw a man named Matthew sitting at
the tax office. And He said to him, "Follow
Me." So he arose and followed Him.*

MATTHEW 9:9

In Jesus' day tax collectors were despised more than
any other group. Even today, no one especially enjoys
paying taxes, but in first-century Israel, tax collectors—
sometimes called publicans—were considered traitors,
and they were hated more than the occupying Romans.

Publicans were men who had bought tax franchises
from the Roman emperor and then extorted money
from the people of Israel to feed the Roman coffers and
pad their own pockets. Obviously, tax collectors had a
certain amount that was legitimate to collect for the

government (cf. Matthew 22:21; Romans 13:7). But there was an unspoken agreement with the Roman emperor that they could assess whatever other fees and additional taxes they could collect, and they were allowed to keep a percentage for themselves. Tax collectors often strong-armed money out of people with the use of thugs. Most were despicable, vile, unprincipled scoundrels. And yet, Jesus chose one of these publicans to be His disciple.

"As Jesus passed on from [Capernaum], He saw a man named Matthew sitting at the tax office. And He said to him, 'Follow Me.' So he arose and followed Him" (Matthew 9:9). It must have been a stunning reality to Matthew when Jesus chose him. It came out of the blue. Jesus simply said, "Follow Me," and Matthew instantly and without hesitation did so. He abandoned the tax office. He left his toll booth and walked away from his cursed profession forever.

The decision was irreversible as soon as he made it. There was no shortage of money-grubbing piranhas who coveted a tax franchise like Matthew's, and as soon as he stepped away, you can be sure someone else stepped in and took over. Once Matthew walked away, he could never go back. Nor did he ever regret his decision.

What was it in a man like Matthew that caused him

to drop everything at once like that? We might assume he was a materialist. And at one time he must have been, or he never would have gotten into a position like that in the first place. So why would he walk away from every-thing and follow Jesus, not knowing what the future held? The best answer we can deduce is that what-ever Matthew's tortured soul may have experienced because of the profession he had chosen, down deep inside he was a Jew who knew and loved the Old Testament. He was spiritually hungry. At some point in his life, most likely after he had chosen his despicable career, he was smitten with a gnawing spiritual hunger and became a true seeker. Of course, God was seeking and drawing him, and the draw was irresistible.

> Most tax collectors were despicable, vile, unprin-cipled scoundrels. And yet, Jesus chose one of these publicans to be His disciple.

We can be certain that Matthew knew the Old Testament very well, because his gospel quotes the Old Testament some ninety-nine times. That is more than Mark, Luke, and John combined. Matthew obviously had extensive familiarity with the Hebrew Scriptures. In fact, he quotes out of the Law, out of the Psalms, and out of the Prophets—every section of the Old Testament. He must have pursued his study on his own, because as a tax collector, he was barred from entering any synagogue. Apparently, in a quest to fill the spiritual void in his life, he had turned to the Scriptures.

Matthew believed in the true God. And because he knew the record of God's revelation, he understood the promises of the Messiah. So when Jesus showed up and called Mathew to follow Him, Matthew had enough faith to drop everything and follow. Matthew's faith is clearly indicated not only in the immediacy of his response but also in the fact that after following Jesus, Matthew held an evangelistic banquet in his home.

Matthew invited a large number of his fellow tax collectors and various other kinds of scoundrels and social outcasts to meet Jesus. His first impulse after becoming a disciple of Jesus was to bring his closest friends and introduce them to the Savior. He was so thrilled to have found the Messiah that he wanted to introduce Jesus to everyone he knew.

As a tax collector, Matthew knew his sin. But when Jesus called him, he understood there was, inherent in that call, the promise of forgiveness. In that, Matthew models true Christian conversion. Before we can receive the grace and forgiveness of God, we too must recognize our great need for a Savior.

Why were tax collectors so hated by their own countrymen?

_____

_____

_____

What was Matthew's response upon hearing Christ's call? How is your heart responding to His ongoing call to faithfulness? Reflect on what Matthew knew he was giving up compared to what he was gaining.

_____

_____

_____

Even before his conversion, where did Matthew seek the Messiah? How did this preparation benefit him after salvation? As a believer, how do you demonstrate at least the same diligence?

_____

_____

_____

Thomas

And Thomas answered and said to Him,
"My Lord and my God!"

JOHN 20:28

He is usually nicknamed "Doubting Thomas," but that label isn't quite fair. Thomas, the disciple of Jesus, was a better man than popular retellings let on.

It probably is fair, however, to say that Thomas was a somewhat negative person. He was a worrywart, a brooder. He tended to be anxious and angst-ridden, not unlike Eeyore in the Winnie the Pooh stories. He anticipated the worst all the time. Pessimism, rather than doubt, seems to have been his besetting sin.

This tendency of Thomas to focus on the downside can be clearly seen in John 11. Jesus and the disciples had received word that Lazarus had fallen ill. Rather than rushing to the aid of His friend, Jesus decided to stay put for two whole days. He deliberately tarried to give Lazarus time to die. Why? Because "Jesus loved Martha and her sister [Mary] and Lazarus" (v. 5). Jesus' delay was an act of love, because ultimately, the blessing they received when Lazarus was raised from the dead was a greater blessing than if he had merely been healed of his sickness. It glorified Jesus in a greater way. It strengthened their faith in Him immeasurably more.

When the two days of waiting were over, Jesus announced to His disciples, "Let us go to Judea again" (v. 7). The disciples thought this was crazy. They frankly did not want to go back to Jerusalem. The ministry in the wilderness was phenomenal. In Jerusalem they all risked being stoned. Now was not a good time for a visit to Bethany, which was virtually within sight of the temple, where Jesus' bitterest enemies had their headquarters.

Jesus was resolute. He was going back to Judea. There was no talking Him out of it. Thomas, recognizing this, said to the other disciples, "Let us also go, that we may die with Him" (v. 16). Now that was pessimistic, and that was typical for Thomas. But it was a heroic pessimism. He was convinced Jesus was heading straight for a stoning. But if that is what the Lord was determined to do, Thomas was grimly determined to go and die with Him. You have to admire his courage.

Thomas's profound love for the Lord shows up again in John 14. Jesus was telling them of His imminent departure. In verse 5 Thomas responds, "Lord, we do not know where You are going, and how can we know the way?" Again we see his pessimism. In essence, he was saying, "You're leaving. We'll never get where You are going. We don't even know how to get there. If we died together, we would all be together. But if You just go, how are we ever going to find You? We don't even know how to get there."

Thomas is a man whose relationship with Christ was so strong that he never wanted to be severed from Him. His heart was broken as he heard Jesus speak of leaving them. He was shattered. And his worst fears came to pass: Jesus died, and he didn't.

We pick up the next picture of Thomas in John 20. After Jesus' death, all the disciples were in deep sorrow. But they all got together to comfort one another. Except for Thomas. He missed the whole thing. "The other disciples therefore said to him, 'We have seen the Lord'" (v. 25).

They were exuberant. They were ecstatic. They were eager to share the good news with Thomas. But someone like Thomas was not going to be cheered up so easily. This news was just too good to be true. "So he said to them, 'Unless I see in His hands the print of the nails, and put my finger into the print of the nails, and put my hand into His side, I will not believe'" (v. 25).

> Thomas is a man whose relationship with Christ was so strong that he never wanted to be severed from Him.

Eight days later, Jesus appeared to the disciples again. This time, Thomas was there. Seeing the resurrected Jesus shattered his pessimism in an instant, and he uttered perhaps the greatest statement ever to come from the lips of the apostles: "My Lord and my God!" (v. 28).

Thomas was a tenderhearted, moody, melancholy individual. But he was transformed by Christ. Are you beginning to get the idea of what kind of people God uses? He can use anyone. Personality, status, and family background are all immaterial. The one thing needed is a willingness to acknowledge our own sinfulness and our need for the grace of God.

Fill out the details of Thomas's specific tendency toward pessimism. What positive traits did he manifest at the same time?

_____

_____

_____

Explain how Jesus' delay in reaching Bethany was an act of love.

_____

_____

_____

Meditate on Thomas's famous confession. When was the last time you were so struck with the truth of Christ that you were prompted to confess the same?

_____

_____

_____

James the Less

. . . Andrew, Philip, Bartholomew,
Matthew, Thomas, James son of Alphaeus,
Thaddaeus, Simon the Canaanite . . .

MARK 3:18

The only thing Scripture tells us about James, the son of Alphaeus, is his name. If he ever wrote anything, it is lost to history. If he ever asked Jesus any questions or did anything to stand out from the group, Scripture does not record it. He never attained any degree of fame or notoriety. He was not the kind of person who stands out. He was utterly obscure. He even had a common name.

Practically all we know about this James is that he was the son of Alphaeus (Matthew 10:3; Mark 3:18; Luke 6:15; Acts 1:13). In Mark 15:40, we learn that James's mother was named Mary. That verse, together with Matthew 27:56 and Mark 15:47 mention another of this woman's sons, Joses.

Aside from these scant details that can be gleaned about his family, James is utterly obscure. His lack of prominence is even reflected in his nickname. In Mark 15:40 he is referred to as "James the Less." The Greek word for *Less* is *mikros*. It literally means "little." Its primary meaning is "small in stature," so it could refer to his physical features. Perhaps he was a short or small-framed man. The word can also speak of someone who is young in age. He might have been younger than James the son of Zebedee, so this title would distinguish him as the younger of the two. But the name most likely refers to his influence.

It may well be that all these things were true of James, so that he was a small, young, quiet person who stayed mostly in the background. That would all be consistent with the low profile he had among the Twelve. We might say his distinguishing mark was his obscurity. That in itself is a significant fact. Apparently he sought no recognition. He displayed no great leadership. He asked no critical questions. He demonstrated no unusual insight. Only his name remains, while his life and his labors are immersed in obscurity.

According to Mark 2:14, Levi, also known as Matthew, was the son of a man named Alphaeus as well. It could be that James was the brother of Matthew.

Scripture doesn't expressly tell us. Had that been important, Scripture would have recorded it for us. What made the apostles important was the Lord whom they served and the message they proclaimed. If we lack details about the men themselves, that is okay. Heaven will reveal the full truth of who they were and what they were like. In the meantime, it is enough to know that they were chosen by the Lord, empowered by the Spirit, and used by God to carry the gospel to the world of their day.

> Scripture always keeps the focus on the power of Christ and the power of the Word, not on the men who were merely instruments of that power.

Most of the disciples more or less disappear from the biblical narrative within a few years after Pentecost. In no case does Scripture give us a full biography. That is because Scripture always keeps the focus on the power of Christ and the power of the Word, not on the men who were merely instruments of that power. These men were filled with the Spirit, and they preached the Word. That is all we really need to know. The vessel is not the issue; the Master is.

There is nothing wrong with being behind the scenes, quiet, and unobtrusive. In fact, it is often the people who love and labor in the background who make the greatest kingdom impact for eternity. The world may not remember much about such people, but their full reward is waiting in eternity.

What can we make of James's comparative obscurity?

_____

_____

_____

What made James truly great?

_____

_____

_____

What does James's lack of eminence tell you about how God chooses to work?

_____

_____

_____

Simon the Zealot

*. . . Matthew and Thomas; James the
son of Alphaeus, and Simon called the
Zealot . . .*

LUKE 6:15

The historian Josephus described four basic parties among the Jews of the first century. The Pharisees were fastidious about the Law; they were the religious fundamentalists of their time. The Sadducees were religious liberals; they denied the supernatural. They were also rich, aristocratic, and powerful. They were in charge of the temple. The Essenes are not mentioned in Scripture at all, but Josephus describes them as ascetics and celibates who lived in the desert and devoted their lives to the study of the Law. The fourth group, the Zealots, were more politically minded than any group of the time besides the Herodians (those who supported the house and dynasty of Herod the Great).

The Zealots hated the Romans, and their goal was to overthrow the Roman occupation. They advanced their agenda primarily through terrorism and surreptitious acts of violence. The Zealots were extremists in every sense. Like the Pharisees, they interpreted the Law literally. Unlike the Pharisees (who were willing to compromise for political reasons), the Zealots were militant, violent outlaws. They believed only God Himself had the right to rule over the Jews. And therefore they believed they were doing God's work by assassinating Roman soldiers, political leaders, and anyone else who opposed them.

The Zealots were hoping for a Messiah who would lead them in overthrowing the Romans and restore the kingdom to Israel with its Solomonic glory. They were red-hot patriots, ready to die in an instant for what they believed.

Many historians believe that when the Romans sacked Jerusalem under Titus Vespasian in AD 70, that terrible holocaust was largely precipitated by the Zealots. During the siege, after the Roman army had already surrounded the city and cut off supplies, the Zealots actually began killing fellow Jews who wanted to negotiate with Rome to end the conflict. When Titus saw how hopeless the situation was, he destroyed the city, massacring thousands of its inhabitants, and carried off the treasures of the temple. So the Zealots' blind hatred of Rome and everything Roman ultimately provoked the destruction of their own city. The spirit of their movement was an insane and self-destructive fanaticism.

Among Jesus' disciples, there was a former Zealot—Simon. We don't know much about him, only that he was identified as a Zealot. For whatever reason—perhaps his fiery personality—the label stuck long after he'd cut formal ties with the group.

It is interesting that when Matthew and Mark list the Twelve, they list Simon just before Judas Iscariot. When Jesus sent the disciples out two by two in Mark 6:7, it is likely that Simon and Judas Iscariot were a team. They probably both originally followed Christ for similar political reasons. But somewhere along the line, Simon became a genuine believer and was transformed. Judas Iscariot never really believed.

Of course, as one of the Twelve, Simon also had to associate with Matthew, who was at the opposite end of the political spectrum, collecting taxes for the Roman government. At one point in his life, Simon would probably have gladly killed Matthew. In the end, they became spiritual brethren, working side by side for the same cause—the spread of the gospel—and worshiping the same Lord.

It is amazing that Jesus would select a man like Simon to be an apostle. But he was a man of fierce loyalties, amazing passion, courage, and zeal. Simon believed the truth and embraced Christ as his Lord. The fiery enthusiasm he once had for Israel was now expressed in his devotion to Christ.

> The fiery enthusiasm Simon once had for Israel was now expressed in his devotion to Christ.

Several early sources say that after the destruction of Jerusalem, Simon took the gospel north and preached in the British Isles. Like so many of the other disciples, Simon simply disappears from the biblical narrative. There is no reliable record of what happened to him, but all accounts say he was killed for preaching the gospel. This man who was once willing to kill and be killed for a political agenda within the confines of Judea found a more fruitful cause for which to give his life: the proclamation of salvation to sinners out of every nation, tongue, and tribe.

Radical passion and devotion, when applied to anything or anyone other than Jesus Christ, can be dangerous. But when that fervor is surrendered to the Savior, it can turn the angriest of political activists into a mighty man or woman of God.

What did Simon originally hope the Messiah's manner of coming would be like?

_____

_____

_____

Consider Simon and Matthew's unity in Christ. How have you seen the same sort of reconciliation in your own life and congregation? Can you think of someone you need to pursue reconciliation with?

_____

_____

_____

Can you identify any areas of misdirected zeal in your life? How can you better align your passions with God's?

_____

_____

_____

Judas

*Judas (not Iscariot) said to Him, "Lord,
how is it that You will manifest Yourself
to us, and not to the world?"*

JOHN 14:22

The name *Judas*, in and of itself, is a fine name. It means "praised." But because of the treachery of Judas Iscariot, the name will forever bear a negative connotation. So when the apostle John mentions another of Jesus' twelve disciples named Judas, he calls him "Judas (not Iscariot)" (John 14:22).

As is the case with most of the first disciples, Scripture doesn't tell us much about Judas, the son of James. Much of what we can glean about him from the Gospels comes to us from his name—or, rather, his three names.

In Matthew 10:3, he is called "Lebbaeus, whose surname was Thaddaeus." *Judas* was probably the name given him at birth. *Lebbaeus* and *Thaddaeus* were essentially nicknames. *Thaddaeus* means "breast child" and evokes the idea of a nursing baby. It almost has a derisive sound, something akin to the modern "mama's boy." Perhaps he was the youngest in his family, and therefore the baby among several siblings—specially cherished by his mother. His other name, *Lebbaeus*, is similar. It is from a Hebrew root that refers to the heart—literally, "heart child." Both names suggest Judas had a tender, childlike heart. It is interesting to think of such a gentle soul hanging around in the same group of apostles as Simon the Zealot. But the Lord can use both kinds. Zealots make great preachers. But so do tenderhearted, compassionate, gentle, sweet-spirited souls like Lebbaeus Thaddaeus. When considered together, the twelve apostles are a very complex and intriguing group. There's at least one of every imaginable personality.

The New Testament records one incident involving this Judas Lebbaeus Thaddaeus. During the Upper Room Discourse, Jesus says, "He who has My commandments and keeps them, it is he who loves Me. And he who loves Me will be loved by My Father, and I will love him and manifest Myself to him."

> When considered together, the twelve apostles are a very complex and intriguing group. There's at least one of every imaginable personality.

Then John adds, "Judas (not Iscariot) said to Him, 'Lord, how is it that You will manifest Yourself to us, and not to the world?'" (John 14:22). Here we see the tenderhearted humility of this man. He doesn't say anything brash or bold or overconfident. He doesn't rebuke the Lord like Peter once did. His question is full of gentleness and meekness and devoid of any sort of pride. He couldn't believe that Jesus would manifest Himself to this ragtag group of eleven, and not to the whole world.

After all, Jesus was the Savior of the world. He was the rightful heir of the earth—King of kings and Lord of lords. They had always assumed that He came to set up His kingdom and subdue all things to Himself. The good news of forgiveness and salvation was certainly good news for all the world. And the disciples knew it well, but the rest of the world was still, by and large, clueless. So Lebbaeus Thaddaeus wanted to know, "Why are You going to disclose Yourself to us and not to the whole world?"

This was a pious, believing disciple. This was a man who loved his Lord and who felt the power of salvation in his own life. He was full of hope for the world, and in his own tenderhearted, childlike way he wanted to know why Jesus wasn't going to make Himself known to everyone. He was obviously still hoping to see the kingdom come to earth. We certainly can't fault him for that; that is how Jesus taught His disciples to pray (Luke 11:2).

Jesus gave him a marvelous answer, and the answer was as tender as the question. "If anyone loves Me, he will keep My word; and My Father will love him, and We will come to him and make Our home with him" (John 14:23). Christ would manifest Himself to anyone who loves Him. Judas was still thinking in the political and material realm, but Jesus was telling him, "I'm going to take over hearts, one at a time."

God certainly uses people who are bold and brash and ready to conquer the world—but He also uses people like Judas Lebbaeus Thaddaeus. That disciple's childlike, kind heart was precious in the sight of Jesus. Judas was not one for the spotlight. He wasn't the most vocal of the apostles. He was a rather ordinary person—proof that God can, and does, use perfectly ordinary people to accomplish His purposes.

Contemplate the twelve apostles' diversity of personalities and backgrounds. How is this reflected in your own experience among Christ's people?

_____

_____

_____

What does Jesus' response to Judas's question tell us about how God deals with us?

_____

_____

_____

How did Christ transform Judas's hope? How does this give you hope?

_____

_____

_____

12 Judas Iscariot

Then Judas Iscariot, one of the twelve,
went to the chief priests to betray Him
to them.

MARK 14:10

He is the most colossal failure in human history. He committed the most horrible, heinous act of any individual, ever. He betrayed the perfect, sinless, holy Son of God for a handful of money. His dark story is a poignant example of the depths to which the human heart is capable of sinking. He spent three years with Jesus Christ, but for all that time his heart was only growing hard and hateful.

While the other eleven apostles are all great encouragements to us because they exemplify how common people with typical failings can be used by God in uncommon, remarkable ways, Judas stands as a warning about the evil potential of spiritual carelessness, squandered opportunity, sinful lusts, and hardness of the heart. Here was a man who drew as close to the Savior as humanly possible. He enjoyed every privilege Christ affords. He was intimately familiar with everything Jesus taught. Yet he remained in unbelief and went into a hopeless eternity.

Judas was ordinary in every way, just like the others. It is significant that when Jesus predicted one of them would betray Him, no one pointed the finger of suspicion at Judas (Matthew 26:22–23). He was so expert in his hypocrisy that no one seemed to distrust him. But Jesus knew his heart from the beginning (John 6:64).

The call of Judas is not recorded in Scripture. It is obvious, however, that he followed Jesus willingly. He was probably a young, zealous, patriotic Jew who did not want the Romans to rule and who hoped Christ would overthrow the foreign oppressors and restore the kingdom to Israel. He obviously could see that Jesus had powers like no other man. There was plenty of reason for a man like Judas to be attracted to that.

It is equally obvious, however, that Judas was not

attracted to Christ on a spiritual level. He was not interested in the kingdom for salvation's sake or for Christ's sake. He was interested only in what he could get out of it. Wealth, power, and prestige were what fueled his ambitions.

At the same time, we must remember that Scripture says Jesus chose Judas. He *knew* Judas would be the one to fulfill the prophecies of betrayal. He knowingly chose him to fulfill the plan. And yet Judas was in no sense coerced into doing what he did. No invisible hand forced him to betray Christ. He acted freely and without external compulsion. He was responsible for his own actions.

> Judas was sorry, not because he had sinned against Christ, but because his sin did not satisfy him the way he had hoped.

Jesus said he would bear the guilt of his deed throughout eternity. His own greed, his own ambition, and his own wicked desires were the only forces that constrained him to betray Christ.

Judas sold Jesus for a pittance, agreeing to lead His enemies to a place where Jesus could be arrested without the interference of the crowds. With a kiss on the cheek, Judas betrayed the King of glory. But as soon as Jesus was taken away and His fate was sealed, Judas's conscience immediately came alive. He found himself in a hell of his own making, hammered by his own mind for what he had done. The money, which had been so important to him before, now did not matter. Matthew 27:3–4 says, "Then Judas, His betrayer, seeing that He had been condemned, was remorseful and brought back the thirty pieces of silver to the chief priests and elders, saying, 'I have sinned by betraying innocent blood.'"

His remorse was not the same as repentance, as subsequent events clearly show. He was sorry, not because he had sinned against Christ, but because his sin did not satisfy him the way he had hoped. In that, Judas's life is truly the saddest of all the lives we encounter in the pages of Scripture.

However, as tragic as it was, the life of Judas does offer us something truly valuable. It serves as a vivid reminder that no matter how sinful a person may be, no matter what treachery he or she may attempt against the Lord, the purposes of God cannot be thwarted. God's sovereign plan cannot be overthrown even by the most cunning schemes of those who hate Him. That is indeed a tremendous comfort to those of us who love the Lord and have placed our undivided trust in His good promises.

What drew Judas to Christ? In examining your own motives, do you find any kinship within them to Judas's? Why or why not?

_____

_____

_____

Explain the difference between the remorse Judas experienced and true repentance—for instance, as pictured by the remorse the apostle Peter experienced. Which is more familiar to your own heart?

_____

_____

_____

How does even Judas Iscariot's life remain an encouragement? Examine it in regard to God's sovereignty.

_____

_____

_____

Eve

*And Adam called his wife's name Eve,
because she was the mother of all the
living.*

GENESIS 3:20

She was the final work of creation, its pinnacle. In her original state, undefiled by any evil, unblemished by any disease or defect, unspoiled by any imperfection at all, Eve was the flawless archetype of feminine excellence. She was magnificent in every way. And yet, Scripture does not offer us a single detail about her appearance. Instead, the Bible's focus is on Eve as "the mother of all the living" (Genesis 3:20).

Eve was Adam's complement in every sense, designed by God to be the ideal soul companion for him. She enjoyed unparalleled intimacy with her husband, having been made for him and from him (Genesis 2:21–22). Although Eve was spiritually and intellectually Adam's peer—they were both of one essence and therefore equals in their standing before God and in their rank above the other creatures—there was nonetheless a clear distinction in their earthly roles. And this was by God's own deliberate creative design.

Adam was created first; then Eve was made to fill a void in his existence. Adam was the head; Eve was his helper. Adam was designed to be a father, provider, protector, and leader. Eve was designed to be a mother, comforter, nurturer, and helper. But we don't get the chance to see Eve live out her divinely designed role in a world without sin, for almost as soon as we meet her in Genesis 2, we are thrust into Genesis 3 and the story of her temptation at the wiles of the serpent, whom Scripture later reveals to be Satan (Revelation 12:9; 20:2).

The devil, as we might expect, twisted the meaning of God's Word: "Has God indeed said, 'You shall not eat of every tree of the garden?'" (Genesis 3:1). God's commandment had actually come to Adam as a positive statement: "Of every tree of the garden you may freely eat; but of the tree of the knowledge of good and evil you shall not eat" (2:16–17). But in the innocent bliss of Eden, Eve was unaware that any danger like this existed. She likely did not know about the possibility of half-truths and questions designed to confuse.

Satan went on to confound Eve with his version of what would happen if she ate: "God knows that in the day you eat of it your eyes will be opened, and you will be like God, knowing good and evil" (3:5).

> Although Eve was spiritually and intellectually Adam's peer, there was nonetheless a clear distinction in their earthly roles. And this was by God's own deliberate creative design.

This was a partial truth. If Eve ate, her eyes certainly would be open to the knowledge of good and evil, but only because she would be forfeiting her innocence.

In the end, Eve was deceived. She "saw that the tree was good for food, that it was pleasant to the eyes, and a tree desirable to make one wise" (v. 6). She ate and then gave to her husband to eat. Even though Eve sinned first, Adam's place of headship in the original family—and therefore the entire human race—led to the fall of humanity. When Adam sinned, he sinned as our representative before God.

Still, Eve was guilty, and she soon discovered the serpent was right about one thing: she now knew good and evil. Unfortunately, she knew evil by experiencing it—by becoming a willing participant in sin. And in that moment, her innocence was gone. The result was agonizing shame.

That shame was soon compounded by the curse placed on the woman: pain in bearing children and an unrelenting desire to upend the God-ordained role given to her in her marriage. But as God was speaking the consequences of sin over Adam, Eve, and the serpent, there was a glimmer of hope given—and Eve grabbed hold of it. God told the serpent, "I will put enmity . . . between your seed and her Seed; He shall bruise your head, and you shall bruise His heel" (v. 15). There it was—"Her Seed"! Eve would get to bear children and raise a family after all. More than that, she now understood that one of her own offspring would destroy the destroyer. She had God's word that, one day, the curse would come undone.

As we know, the "Seed" God spoke of was His own Son, who would be born of a woman and thus become one of Eve's descendants. Jesus was Eve's hope—and He's our hope as well, no matter how devastating our personal failings or their consequences.

*Name the traits Scripture gives us in showing how
Eve was the pinnacle of feminine excellence. Do you
look to the same standards in your own estimation
of what constitutes an exemplary woman? What
have you added or removed, and why?*

---

*Contemplate the role of partial truths in the story
of the fall of mankind. What implications can you
draw from that reflection for your own life?*

---

*How do we see Eve's faith in God's promise by her
proceeding to fulfill God's designated role for her,
even after the devastation of the Fall? Consider
how you respond immediately after you sin.*

Sarah

And Sarah said, "God has made me laugh, and all who hear will laugh with me."

GENESIS 21:6

When we meet Sarai (later renamed Sarah), we're told something that sums up everything Scripture has to say about the first sixty-five years of Sarah's life: "Sarai was barren; she had no child" (Genesis 11:30). From the time she became Abraham's wife, Sarah desired one thing above all others, and that was to have children.

Sarah was obviously tortured by her childlessness. Every recorded episode of ill temper or strife in her household was related to her frustrations about her own barrenness. It ate at her. She spent years in the grip of frustration and depression because of it. She desperately wanted to be a mother, but she finally concluded that God Himself was restraining her from having children (16:2).

The Lord's purpose in calling Abraham was to make him the father of a great nation that would be His witness to the world. Sarah obviously had a key role to play in this plan. Abraham could never become the patriarch of a great nation if she did not first become mother to his offspring. She was surely aware of the Lord's promises to her husband. She certainly longed to see those promises fulfilled. As long as she remained childless, however, the sense that everything somehow hinged on her must have felt like a great burden on her shoulders.

So badly did Sarah want her husband to have an heir that she concocted a scheme that was immoral, unrighteous, and utterly foolish. She rashly persuaded Abraham to father a child by her own housemaid. It was a scheme that was so ill-advised and so completely fleshly that Sarah regretted it for the rest of her days. To be fair, from a purely human viewpoint, we can understand Sarah's despair. If God planned to make her the mother of Abraham's heir, why had He not done so by now? It was natural for her to think God was deliberately withholding children from her. As a matter of fact, He was. His plan all along was for Sarah to have her first child in her old age, after every prospect of a natural fulfillment of the prophecy was exhausted and after every earthly reason for hope was completely dead. In this way, the Lord would put His power on full display.

In Sarah's earthly reasoning, Abraham *had* to father children by some means. She thus took it upon herself to try to engineer a fulfillment of the divine promise to Abraham. In doing so, she unwittingly stepped into a role that belonged only to God.

> Sarah laughed in bitterness when she overheard the Lord telling her husband that she would soon be pregnant. She laughed again in joy after she held her son, Isaac, in her arms.

Sarah gave her maidservant to her husband, probably thinking that since she owned Hagar, any children born could be reckoned as her own. Regrettably, her plan worked. Hagar conceived and gave Abraham a son. The consequences of this one act of faithlessness on Sarah's part had unbelievably far-reaching implications. Frankly, some of the tensions we see in the Middle East today are rooted in Sarah's foolhardy ploy.

Thirteen more frustrating years passed for Sarah after Hagar gave birth to Ishmael. At eighty-nine years old, Sarah remained barren. She had lived in Canaan for twenty-four years, and her husband was about to have his hundredth birthday. If her hope was not utterly shattered, it must have hung by a very thin thread. But here's where the greatness of Sarah's faith shines through. She had harbored hope for so long. Year after year had come and gone. She was now an old woman, and no matter how often she and Abraham tried to conceive, the promise was still unfulfilled. Most women would have given up long before this. A lesser woman might have despaired of ever seeing the Lord's promise fulfilled and turned to paganism instead. But we are reminded again that Sarah "judged Him faithful who had promised" (Hebrews 11:11). This is what made her so extraordinary.

Sarah laughed in bitterness when she overheard the Lord telling her husband that she would soon be pregnant. She laughed again in joy after she held her son, Isaac, in her arms. This laughter tells us something important about Sarah: Despite her occasional bursts of temper and struggles with discouragement, Sarah remained an essentially good-humored woman. After those long years of bitter frustration, she could still appreciate the irony and relish the comedy of becoming a mother at such an old age.

God is faithful to keep His promises. Like Sarah, we must be faithful to trust in them.

Put yourself in Sarah's position, bearing in mind all her cultural and historical context. When are you tempted not to trust the Lord and instead to take matters into your own hands? Do you more consistently make excuses for this attitude or repent of it?

_____

_____

_____

How well are you doing entrusting your desires to the Lord and waiting on His timing for you? How does Sarah's history encourage you, both positively and negatively, to that end?

_____

_____

_____

Sarah

What does Hebrews 11:11 tell us about Sarah?
Memorize verses 11 and 12 as weapons against
your own moments of wavering.

_____

_____

_____

71

Rahab

Now therefore, I beg you, swear to me by the Lord, since I have shown you kindness, that you also will show kindness to my father's house.

JOSHUA 2:12

Jericho was on the brink of judgment. The city's long descent into the abyss of moral and spiritual corruption had been intentional, and now it was irreversible. God had determined Jericho's time was up; the city and its people would soon be destroyed.

It's hard to imagine courageous faith could be found in such a dark place, but Rahab's story proves otherwise. Prior to the events of Joshua 2, Rahab was a prostitute living comfortably within the walls of a decadent, pagan city. As far as we know, Rahab had always been a willing participant in her civilization's trademark debauchery. She had personally profited from the evil that permeated that whole society.

As far as the record of her life is concerned, there were no redeeming qualities whatsoever about Rahab's life up to this point. On the contrary, she would have been in the very basement of the moral hierarchy in a Gentile culture that was itself as thoroughly degenerate and as grossly pagan as any society in world history. She was a moral bottom-feeder. She made her living off that culture's insatiable appetite for unbridled debauchery, catering to the most debased appetites of the very dregs of society. Yet, despite Rahab's deplorable background, she is specifically singled out by name for the greatness of her faith in Hebrews 11:31, and she even appears in the family tree of Jesus in Matthew 1.

The turning point of Rahab's life came when two Israelite spies showed up at her door. She knew all about the Israelites and the God they worshiped. All of Jericho had heard about Israel's miraculous escape from the pharaoh across the Red Sea and the drowning of the entire Egyptian army (Joshua 2:10). The story of Israel's subsequent wanderings in the wilderness was also well known throughout the region. In Rahab's own words, "As soon as we heard these things, our hearts melted; neither did there remain any more courage in anyone because of you" (v. 11).

This initial fear of the Lord sparked within Rahab a small flame of faith. While she certainly could have turned the spies in and received a handsome reward— after all, she had made her living selling herself for immoral purposes—she instead chose to shift her loyalty from her people and their false gods to Israel and the one, true God.

When soldiers came looking for the spies, she hid them and then lied to throw the men off their trail. We may ask whether her lying was justified. Good men have argued over that question, all the way back to the earliest rabbinical history. The important thing to note is that Scripture never commends the lie. Instead, Rahab is lauded as a positive example of faith. Even though, at that moment, her faith was newborn, weak, and in need of nurture and growth—as small as a mustard seed, some might say—it was genuine faith in the Lord.

The spies swore an oath to deal kindly with her when they conquered her city. But they gave her one condition. She was to hang a scarlet cord from the window where

she let them down (vv. 17–18).
The color would make it easily
visible from beneath the wall.
Both its appearance and its
function were reminiscent of
the crimson sign of the blood
sprinkled on the doorposts at

> Rahab is extra-
> ordinary precisely
> because she received
> extraordinary grace.

the first Passover. Many believe the scarlet color also
points forward to the blood of Jesus Christ, the true
Paschal Lamb.

Rahab is a beautiful example of the transforming
power of faith. Although she had few spiritual advantages
and little knowledge of the truth, her heart was drawn to
the Lord. She risked her life, turned her back on a way
of life that did not honor God, and walked away from
everything but her closest family members (whom she
brought into the community of God's people along with
her). From that day on, she lived a completely different
kind of life, as a true hero of faith.

Rahab is extraordinary precisely because she received
extraordinary grace. Though some have tried, there's no
need to reinvent her past to try to make her seem less of
a sinner. The fact of who she once was simply magnifies
the glory of divine grace in her life. In that, there is a

lesson for all of us: no matter where we may have come from or what we may have done in the past, the grace of God brings new life.

Despite her personal history and lingering instinct to lie, what does Scripture focus on and commend Rahab for (cf. Heb. 11:31)?

_____

_____

_____

Meditate on the grace of God that made Rahab truly extraordinary. How do you see the same grace functioning in yourself?

_____

_____

_____

How does Rahab's narrative instruct us on how we should biblically view our own sinful pasts?

_____

_____

_____

Ruth

Your people shall be my people, and
your God, my God.

RUTH 1:16

The story of Ruth begins with a man named Elimelech,
his wife, Naomi, and their two sons, Mahlon and Chilion.
Though Elimelech and his family were devout Israelites,
a famine in Israel forced them to seek refuge in Moab.
These must have been desperate times, because Moab
itself was a mostly desolate region.

Not only was the land of Moab arid, it was spiritually
parched as well. Moabite worship was centered around
a god they called Chemosh and was filled with erotic
imagery and lewd conduct. At times it could even involve
human sacrifice (2 Kings 3:26–27). Moabite culture

practically epitomized everything that faithful Israelites were supposed to shun.

Tragedy quickly mounted for Elimelech's family in Moab. First, Elimelech died, leaving Naomi, Mahlon, and Chilion to fend for themselves in a foreign land. Then, shortly after the young men took wives for themselves from among the Moabites (Ruth 1:3–4), they both died too. Now, Naomi was left with her two daughters-in-law, Ruth and Orpah, and together they faced a nearly impossible situation. Three widows, with no children and no responsible relatives, in a time of famine, could not hope to survive for long, even if they pooled their meager resources.

Naomi longed for her homeland and her own people, so she decided to return to Bethlehem. Both daughters-in-law began the difficult journey with her, but as Naomi considered their circumstances, she decided to release them back to their own families. Orpah left Naomi with her blessing, but Ruth refused to leave. Instead, in an expression of extraordinary faith and loyalty, she said, "Wherever you go, I will go; and wherever you lodge, I will lodge; your people shall be my people, and your God, my God" (v. 16).

In agreeing to return to Bethlehem with Naomi,

Ruth was agreeing to help support the aging woman. Ruth was still quite young and physically strong, so when they arrived in Bethlehem, she went to work in the fields, gleaning what the harvesters left behind in order to provide enough grain to eke out an existence. As it happened, she gleaned a field belonging to Boaz, one of Naomi's close relatives, and he saw her. The language of the text suggests that this was purely by happenstance— "She happened to come to the part of the field belonging to Boaz" (2:3)—but we know from the clear teaching of Scripture that God Himself providentially orchestrated these events (Proverbs 16:33).

When Boaz discovered that this woman was his relative by marriage, he showed her special favor. He encouraged her to glean only in his fields and to stay close by his harvesters. He gave her permission to drink from the water he supplied his servants, and he instructed his young men not to touch her. He also encouraged his workers to let grain fall purposely from the bundles for Ruth's sake. As a result, Ruth brought home a full half-bushel of barley, approximately enough to sustain Ruth and Naomi for five days or more.

That evening, when Ruth told Naomi the man who had been her benefactor was named Boaz, Naomi instantly saw the hand of God in the blessing: "This man is a relation of ours, one of our close relatives" (Ruth 2:20). Boaz was a *goel*, an official guardian of the family's honor. In this case, he had the ability to revive Elimelech's family lineage by marrying Ruth and fathering offspring who would inherit the family name and property.

> Ruth's life is a perfect depiction of the story of redemption, told with living, breathing symbols.

In time—and with prodding from Naomi—Ruth made her feelings and intentions known, and Boaz reciprocated. He met with the elders at the city gate and cleared the way, legally speaking, for the redemption of Elimelech's land and his marriage to Ruth. In this, Boaz became a picture of Christ, our true Kinsman-Redeemer, who paid the price to buy us back from our bondage and redeem our lives.

Ruth's life is a perfect depiction of the story of redemption, told with living, breathing symbols. Ruth was not only an outcast and an exile, but also bereft of any resources—without hope of ever being able to redeem herself by any means. Thus, she is a fitting symbol of every believer, and even of the church itself—redeemed, brought into a position of great favor, endowed with riches and privilege, exalted to be the Redeemer's own bride, and loved by Him with the profoundest affection.

List the main characteristics of Ruth you can glean from the text of Ruth chapters 1–4. How are you pursuing the same virtues?

_____

_____

_____

How is Ruth a symbol of every believer? Of you specifically?

_____

_____

_____

List the ways Boaz's traits and actions resemble Christ.

_____

_____

_____

Hannah

For this child I prayed, and the LORD
has granted me my petition which I
asked of Him.

1 SAMUEL 1:27

Like Sarah before her, Hannah was childless and dis-
traught over it. Both women's marriages were plagued
with stress because of their husbands' bigamy. Both ultimately received the blessing they sought from God, and
in both cases, the answers to their prayers turned out
to be exceedingly and abundantly more significant than
they had ever dared to ask or think. You see, Hannah
lived at a time when Israel was in desperate need of a
great leader. Hannah was the woman God used to shape
that leader.

Hannah obviously had a deep and abiding love for God. She was a devout woman whose affections were set on heavenly things, not on earthly things. Her desire for a child was no mere craving for self-gratification. It wasn't about her. It wasn't about getting what she wanted. It was about self-sacrifice—giving herself to that little life in order to give him back to the Lord.

Centuries earlier, Jacob's wife Rachel had begged, "Give me children, or else I die!" (Genesis 30:1). Hannah's prayer was more modest than that. She did not pray for "children," but for one son. She begged God for one son who would be fit to serve in the tabernacle. If God would give her that son, she would give him back to God.

Hannah's actions proved that she wanted a child not for her own pleasure but because she wanted to dedicate him to the Lord.

> Hannah's desire for a child was no mere craving for self-gratification. It wasn't about her.

Despite her disappointment and heartache, she remained faithful. In fact, frustration seems to have turned her more and more to God, not away from Him. And she persisted in prayer. That's a beautiful characteristic, and it was Hannah's distinctive virtue: constant, steadfast faith.

First Samuel 1:12 speaks of her prayer as continual: "She *continued* praying before the LORD" (emphasis added). She stayed before the Lord, even with a broken heart, pouring out tearful prayers. Her trials had the benefit of making her a woman of prayer. She truly exemplifies what it meant to "pray without ceasing" (1 Thessalonians 5:17; Luke 18:1–8). Truly, the value of persistent and passionate prayer is one of the central lessons we can glean from Hannah's life.

When Hannah and Elkanah returned home from the tabernacle, Scripture says, "Elkanah knew Hannah his wife, and the LORD remembered her. So it came to pass in the process of time that Hannah conceived and bore a son" (1 Samuel 1:19–20). She named him Samuel, but the meaning of *Samuel* is not entirely clear. In Hebrew, the name is very similar to Ishmael, which means, "God shall hear." Whatever the actual significance of the name, the essence of what it meant to Hannah is certain. Samuel was a living answer to prayer and a reminder that God had heard what she asked and granted her heart's desire.

Hannah devoted herself solely to Samuel's care for the next few years. When the time came to make the first trip to Shiloh after the baby's birth, Hannah told her husband she planned to stay at home with Samuel until he was weaned. "Then," she said, "I will take him, that he may appear before the LORD and remain there forever" (v. 22). She knew her time with Samuel would be short. Mothers in that culture nursed their children for approximately three years. She would care for him during his most formative years, while he learned to walk and talk. As soon as he was weaned, though, she was determined to fulfill her vow.

Hannah seemed to understand how vital those early years of a child's life are. She prepared Samuel for a lifetime of service to God—the high calling to which she had consecrated him before he was ever born. History tells us that she did her job well. Samuel, obviously a precocious child, grew in wisdom and understanding. Those early years set a course for his life from which he never deviated.

Scripture says God blessed Hannah with five more children—three sons and two daughters (2:21). Her extraordinary life stands as a wonderful example to women today who want their homes to be places where God is honored, even amid a dark and sinful culture. Her life is also a reminder to all of us that there is no limit to what the Lord can do through one person totally and unreservedly devoted to Him.

How does the biblical text show Hannah's depth of devotion to God? What attitudes and practices in her life evidence that?

_____

_____

_____

What made Hannah's frustration drive her nearer to rather than further from God? Can you say the same for yourself? Why or why not?

_____

_____

_____

What can we learn from Hannah's example of prayer? Use Scripture to support your answers.

_____

_____

_____

Mary of Nazareth

Then Mary said, "Behold the maidservant of the Lord! Let it be to me according to your word."

LUKE 1:38

Of all the extraordinary women in Scripture, one stands out above all others as the most blessed, most highly favored by God, and most universally admired by women. Indeed, no woman is more truly remarkable than Mary. She was the one sovereignly chosen by God—from among all the women who have ever been born—to be the singular instrument through which He would at last bring the Messiah into the world.

When we first meet Mary in Luke's gospel, an angel has appeared to her suddenly and without fanfare to disclose to her God's wonderful plan. Scripture says, simply, "The angel Gabriel was sent by God to a city of Galilee named Nazareth, to a virgin betrothed to a man whose name was Joseph, of the house of David. The virgin's name was Mary" (Luke 1:26–27).

Mary is the equivalent of the Hebrew "Miriam." The name may be derived from the Hebrew word meaning "bitter." Mary's young life may well have been filled with bitter hardships. Her hometown was a forlorn community in a poor district of Galilee. Mary had lived there all her life, in a community where, frankly, good things were probably scarce.

At the time of Gabriel's visit, Mary was probably still a teenager. It was customary for girls in that culture to be betrothed while they were still as young as thirteen years of age. Mary was already formally bound to Joseph, and Scripture is very clear in teaching that Mary was still a virgin when Jesus was miraculously conceived in her womb.

Common sense suggests that Mary must have anticipated the difficulties that would come to her the moment the angel told her she would conceive a child. Still, Mary surrendered herself unconditionally, saying, "Behold the maidservant of the Lord! Let it be to me according to your word" (v. 38). Mary instantly, humbly, and joyfully submitted to God's will without further doubt or question. She could hardly have had a more godly response to the announcement of Jesus' birth. It demonstrated that she was a young woman of mature faith and a worshiper of the true God.

Her heartfelt praise was evident when Mary visited her cousin Elizabeth. Known as the Magnificat, Mary's song is really a hymn about the incarnation. Without question, it is a song of unspeakable joy and the most magnificent psalm of worship in the New Testament. Reading Mary's words of adoration to God, it is clear that Mary's young heart and mind were

> Mary instantly, humbly, and joyfully submitted to God's will without further doubt or question.

already thoroughly saturated with the Word of God. Her worship was clearly from the heart. She was plainly consumed by the wonder of God's grace to her. Mary seemed amazed that an absolutely holy God would do such great things for one as undeserving as she.

As Jesus grew up, Mary was like no other mother. Godly mothers are typically absorbed in the task of training their children for heaven. Mary's Son was the Lord and Creator of heaven. Over time, she came to perceive the full import of that truth until it filled her heart. She became a disciple and a worshiper. Her maternal relationship with Him faded into the background.

When Jesus was dying on the cross, Mary was one of a few disciples who remained by His side. Her sense of the injustice being done to Him must have been profound. After all, no one understood Jesus' absolute, sinless perfection better than Mary did. She had nurtured Him as an infant and brought Him up through childhood. No one could have loved Him more than she did. All those facts merely compounded the acute grief any mother would feel at such a horrible sight. The depth of Mary's anguish is almost unimaginable. Yet she stood, stoically, silently, when lesser women would have fled in horror, shrieked, thrashed around in panic, or simply collapsed in a heap from the overwhelming distress. Mary was clearly a woman of dignified grace and courage.

While we should never venerate Mary the way some traditions do, Mary is worthy of our deepest admiration for no other reason than this: her life and her testimony point us consistently to her Son. *He* was the object of her worship. *He* was the one she recognized as Lord. *He* was the one she trusted for everything. Mary's own example, seen in the pure light of Scripture, teaches us to do the same.

Reflect on the maturity that Mary's replies to the angel Gabriel and her hymn of praise exhibit. How are you cultivating the same mature faith in your own heart, and in the hearts of young believers in your life?

_____

_____

_____

Meditate on the grace and courage Mary exhibited at Christ's crucifixion even as the experience was as a sword piercing her soul (Luke 2:35). What enabled her to endure such circumstances?

_____

_____

_____

Consider Mary's humble adoration of Jesus over a lifetime of knowing Him. Do you, having the still fuller revelation of His glory, live with as much devotion to Him? Why or why not?

_____

_____

_____

Anna 19

And coming in that instant she gave thanks
to the Lord, and spoke of Him to all those
who looked for redemption in Jerusalem.

LUKE 2:38

In the first century, messianic expectations were running at an all-time high. Practically every faithful believer in Israel was waiting with bated breath for the Holy One to make His appearance. The irony is that when Jesus did show up, very few recognized Him. They were looking for a mighty political and military leader who would become a conquering king; He was born into a peasant family. They probably anticipated that He would arrive with great fanfare and pageantry; He was born in a stable, almost in secret.

The only people in Israel who did recognize Christ at His birth were humble, unremarkable people, one of whom was Anna. Everything Scripture has to say about her is contained in just three verses: Luke 2:36–38. She is never mentioned anywhere else in the Bible. But these three verses are enough to establish her reputation as a genuinely extraordinary woman.

Anna's hopes and dreams were full of messianic expectation. She knew the Old Testament promises, and she understood that salvation from sin and the future blessing of Israel depended on the coming of the Messiah. Her longing to see Him was suddenly and surprisingly fulfilled one day as she went about her normal routine in the temple.

Luke introduces her this way: "There was one, Anna, a prophetess" (Luke 2:36). What does Luke mean by *prophetess*? He is not suggesting that Anna predicted the future. He's not necessarily even suggesting she received special revelation from God. Most likely, he means she had a reputation as a gifted teacher of other women and a faithful encourager of her fellow worshipers in the temple. When she spoke, it was about the Word of God. She had evidently spent a lifetime hiding God's Word in her heart. Naturally, that was the substance of what she usually had to say. So when Luke called her a "prophet-ess," he gave insight into her character and a clue about what occupied her mind and her conversation.

Anna is further identified as "the daughter of Phanuel, of the tribe of Asher" (v. 36). Her heritage is given because it was rather unusual. The tribe that descended from Asher belonged to the apostate northern kingdom of Israel. If you remember Old Testament history, you know that the people of that nation were taken into captivity and relocated across the Assyrian Empire.

Anna's descent from the tribe of Asher suggests that her heritage owed much to God's grace. Her ancestors had either migrated south before the Assyrian conquest of Israel, or they were among the small and scattered group of exiles who returned from captivity. Either way, she was part of the believing remnant from the north-ern kingdom, and she was therefore a living emblem of God's faithfulness to His people.

By the time of Jesus' birth, Anna was already advanced in years—"A widow of about eighty-four years" (v. 37). The Greek text here is ambiguous. It may mean that Anna was a widow for eighty-four years or that she was an eighty-four-year-old widow. Either way, she "had lived with a husband seven years" (v. 36) and had lived without him for a long time. Anna probably either lived on charity or supported herself out of the remnants of her family's inheritance. Either way, she must have led a very frugal, chaste, and sober life—and she "served God with fastings and prayers night and day" (v. 37).

Luke tells us Anna came along in the temple courts at just the right moment. When she saw the infant Jesus, she knew in an instant everything she had been praying and fasting for was right there in front of her face, wrapped in a little bundle. It was then that Anna's prophetic giftedness came boldly to the forefront: "[She] spoke of Him to all those who looked for redemption in Jerusalem" (v. 38). The verb tense signifies continuous action. This became her one message for the rest of her life.

> Anna was a wonderfully remarkable woman—perhaps one of the most devout people we meet anywhere on the pages of Scripture.

Anna was a wonderfully remarkable woman—perhaps one of the most devout people we meet anywhere on the pages of Scripture. No one else comes to mind who fasted and prayed faithfully for so many years! And she was rewarded with the greatest blessing there is—Jesus Christ. Let each of us live in such a way that the world around us will know that we, too, live for nothing but Jesus and His glory.

What gave Anna the certainty and expectation of the Messiah? How did the same diligence manifest itself in the ministry that characterized her life and identity?

_____

_____

_____

Explain how Anna was a living reminder of God's faithfulness to His covenant people, Israel.

_____

_____

_____

How does the text communicate to us Anna's joy at encountering Christ? How do you exhibit the same joy in how you speak of Him to others?

_____

_____

_____

The Samaritan Woman

Come, see a Man who told me all thing
that I ever did. Could this be the Christ?

JOHN 4:29

Respectable Jews didn't go to Samaria. In fact, they avoided the region at all costs. For Jesus to be in Samaria at all was unusual (and to His contemporaries even somewhat scandalous).

The Samaritans were a mixed-race people descended from pagans who had intermarried with the few remaining Israelites after the Assyrians conquered the northern kingdom (722 BC). By the first century, the Samaritans had a distinct culture built around a syncretistic religion, blending aspects of Judaism and rank paganism. Their place of worship was on Mount

Gerizim rather than the temple in Jerusalem, and they regarded the Pentateuch (the first five books of the Old Testament) as Scripture but rejected the Psalms and the Prophets. The Jews' contempt for the Samaritans was intense, and yet Jesus chose *this* time and *this* place and *this* woman to be part of the setting where He would (for the first time ever) formally and explicitly unveil His true identity as the Messiah.

Jesus' conversation with the woman at the well started out simply enough—He asked her for a drink. She knew the gender taboos, the racial divisions, and the class system that would normally keep a man of Jesus' status from conversing with a woman like her, so she asked, "How is it that You, being a Jew, ask a drink from me, a Samaritan woman?" (John 4:9).

Bypassing her actual question, Jesus said, "If you knew the gift of God, and who it is who says to you, 'Give Me a drink,' you would have asked Him, and He would have given you living water" (v. 10). He was already hinting at the real message He intended to give her.

As their conversation continued, Jesus invited the woman to go and fetch her husband. Now she was in a quandary. He seemed to be assuming she was a typical woman with a respectable home and an honorable

husband. She was nothing like that. But instead of expos-
ing all her disgrace to this rabbi, she told him only a
small fraction of the truth: "I have no husband" (v. 17).

To the woman's utter chagrin, He knew the full
truth already: "Jesus said to her, 'You have well said, "I
have no husband," for you have had five husbands, and
the one whom you now have is not your husband; in
that you spoke truly'" (vv. 17–18). He knew all about her
sin right down to the infinitesimal details. At this point,
she certainly must have wondered exactly who this was
and how He knew so much about her. But instead of
pursuing that question, she brought up what was to her
mind the biggest point of religious contention between
the Jews and the Samaritans: "Our fathers worshiped on
this mountain, and you Jews say that in Jerusalem is the
place where one ought to worship" (v. 20).

Jesus told her the truth: "The hour is coming, and
now is, when the true worshipers will worship the Father
in spirit and truth; for the Father is seeking such to worship Him" (v. 23).

She replied with these amazing words: "'I know that
Messiah is coming' (who is called Christ). 'When He
comes, He will tell us all things'" (v. 25). She *knew* the
Messiah was coming. That was a definitive expression

of confidence. It was embryonic faith waiting to be born. And how did she think the true Messiah would identify Himself? "When He comes, He will tell us all things." Jesus had already demonstrated His full knowledge of all her secrets.

> The person who has just had the burden of sin and guilt lifted always wants to share the good news with others.

No sooner had she broached the subject of the Messiah than Jesus said, "I who speak to you am He" (v. 26). At this revelation, the woman left the well and returned to the city. The person who has just had the burden of sin and guilt lifted always wants to share the good news with others. The woman's excitement must have been palpable.

Multitudes have come to Christ through the influence of John 4 and "because of the word of the woman who testified, 'He told me all that I ever did'" (v. 39). Only heaven will reveal the vast and far-reaching fruits her encounter with the Messiah wrought. In the meantime, you and I have a testimony about Jesus and the living water He offers. May we be as eager as this Samaritan woman was to share the good news with everyone we know.

Explain why it was so situationally unlikely that Jesus should speak with the Samaritan woman at all. Reflect on some of your recent interactions to answer the following question: Are you content to abide by societal or natural expectations, or do you apply Jesus' standards in deciding who to speak to, and when and why?

_____

_____

_____

How did the Samaritan woman respond to the revelation of who Jesus is? How does that tie directly into her legacy among all who believe?

_____

_____

_____

In as many ways as you can, enumerate how the Samaritan woman's encounter with Jesus exhibits God's grace in salvation.

_____

_____

_____

Mary of Bethany

One thing is needed, and Mary has chosen that good part, which will not be taken away from her.

LUKE 10:42

In the Gospels, Mary is routinely paired with her sister Martha. They lived with their brother, Lazarus, in the small village of Bethany. That was within easy walking distance of Jerusalem, approximately two miles southeast of the temple's eastern gate (John 11:18)—just over the Mount of Olives from Jerusalem's city center. Both Luke and John recorded that Jesus enjoyed hospitality in the home of this family. Bethany was apparently a regular stop for Him in His travels, and this family's home seems to have become a welcome hub for Jesus during His visits to Judea.

Martha and Mary make a fascinating pair—very different in many ways, but alike in one vital respect: both of them loved Christ. Mary's devotion shines particularly bright in one famous episode recorded in three of the Gospels. John 12 (with parallel accounts in Matthew 26:6–13 and Mark 14:3–9) records how Mary anointed the feet of Jesus with costly ointment and wiped His feet with her hair. Both Matthew 26:12 and John 12:7 indicate that Mary, in some sense, understood she was anointing Jesus for burial. She must have strongly suspected that her brother's resurrection would drive Jesus' enemies to a white-hot hatred, and they would be determined to put Him to death (John 11:53–54). Mary seemed to grasp more clearly than anyone how imminent the threat to Jesus was. That surely intensified her sense of debt and gratitude toward Him, as reflected in her act of worship.

With all the disciples present, the dinner party was a sizable one. Perhaps it was a formal celebration of Lazarus's return from the dead. If so, this group of friends had come together mainly to express their gratitude to Jesus for what He had done.

Mary knew exactly how best to show gratitude. Her action of anointing Jesus was strikingly similar to another account from earlier in Jesus' ministry (Luke 7:36–50). At a different gathering, in the home of a different man, a woman "who was a sinner" (v. 37)—apparently a repentant prostitute (v. 39)—had once anointed Jesus' feet and wiped them with her hair, exactly like Mary in the John 12 account. In all likelihood, the earlier incident was well known to Mary. She knew the lesson Jesus taught on that occasion: "Her sins, which are many, are forgiven, for she loved much" (v. 47). Mary's reenactment would therefore have been a deliberate echo of the earlier incident, signifying how much she also loved Jesus and how supremely grateful to Him she was.

> Mary was so consumed with thoughts of Christ that she became completely oblivious to everything else—including all the work Martha was doing to care for their guests.

Mary's singular focus on Jesus was not isolated to this one event either. Earlier, when Jesus visited the home of Mary and Martha, it was Mary who made herself comfortable at Jesus' feet while Martha busied herself with all the work that must be done for guests who have come to call. No doubt Jesus' disciples were asking Him questions, and He was giving answers that were thought-provoking, authoritative, and utterly edifying. Mary's instinct was to sit and listen.

In fact, Mary was so consumed with thoughts of Christ that she became completely oblivious to everything else—including all the work Martha was doing to care for their guests. She sat at the Lord's feet and listened to Him intently, absorbing His every word and nuance. She was by no means being lazy, as her sister, Martha, imagined. She simply understood the true importance of this occasion. The Son of God Himself was a guest in her home. Listening to Him and worshiping Him were, at that moment, the very best use of Mary's energies and the one right place for her to focus her attention.

Mary had "chosen that good part" (Luke 10:42). She had discovered the one thing needful: true worship and devotion of one's heart and full attention to Christ. That was a higher priority even than service, and the good part she had chosen would not be taken away from her, even for the sake of something as gracious and beneficial as helping Martha prepare Jesus a meal. Mary's humble, obedient heart was a far greater gift to Christ than Martha's well-set table.

Mary of Bethany is a much-needed example for us, a reminder that the highest calling we have in this life is to worship and adore the Son of God. May the Lord see us choosing "that good part" time and time again!

Examine Mary's act of worship, as recorded in John 12. What was her primary motivation in performing it?

_____

_____

_____

What was Mary's mindset in the famous incident Luke 10 records? Defend your answer from the text. Can you say you've shared her focus in your recent encounters with God's Word? Why or why not?

_____

_____

_____

Is Luke 10 setting worship and service at odds with each other? What made the difference in the sisters' acts of devotion to Christ?

_____

_____

_____

Martha of Bethany

And Jesus answered and said to her,
"Martha, Martha, you are worried and
troubled about many things."

LUKE 10:41

We're not told how the household of Martha, Mary, and Lazarus became so intimate with Jesus. Since no family ties are ever mentioned between Jesus' relatives and the Bethany clan, it seems likely that Martha and Mary were simply two of the many people who heard Jesus teach early in His ministry, extended Him hospitality, and built a relationship with Him that way. In whatever way this relationship began, it obviously developed into a warm and deeply personal fellowship. It is clear from Luke's description that Jesus made Himself at home in their house.

Certainly hospitality was a special hallmark of this family. Martha in particular is portrayed everywhere as a meticulous hostess. Even her name is the feminine form of the Aramaic word meaning "Lord." It was a perfect name for her because she was clearly the one who presided over her house. Luke 10:38 speaks of the family home as Martha's house. That, together with the fact that her name was usually listed first whenever she was named with her siblings, implies strongly that she was the elder sister.

When Jesus was a guest in her house, Martha fussed over her hostess duties. She wanted everything to be just right. She was a conscientious and considerate hostess, and these are admirable traits. Much in her behavior was commendable. Soon, however, Martha began to notice that her sister, Mary, was not helping her with the necessary chores. She grew irritable with Mary.

> Martha's behavior shows how subtly and sinfully human pride can corrupt even the best of our actions.

It's easy to imagine how Martha's exasperation might have elevated. At first, she probably tried to hint in a "subtle" way that she needed help, perhaps by making extra noise—maybe moving some pots and pans around with a little more vigor than the situation really required and then by letting some utensils or cookware clatter together loudly in a washbasin. Martha might have cleared her throat or exhaled a few times loudly enough to be heard in the next room. Anything to remind Mary that her sister was expecting a little help. When all of that failed, she probably tried to peek around the corner or walk briskly through to the dining room, hoping to catch Mary's eye. In the end, however, she just gave up all pretense of subtlety or civility and aired her grievance against Mary right in front of Jesus. In fact, she complained to Him and asked Him to intervene and set Mary straight.

Martha's behavior shows how subtly and sinfully human pride can corrupt even the best of our actions. What Martha was doing was by no means a bad thing. She was waiting on Christ and her other guests. In a very practical and functional sense, she was acting as servant to all, just as Christ had so often commanded. But the moment she stopped listening to Christ and made something other than Him the focus of her heart and attention, her perspective became very self-centered. At that point, even her service to Christ became tainted with self-absorption and spoiled by a very uncharitable failure to assume the best of her sister. Worst of all, Martha's words impugned the Lord Himself:

"Lord, do You not care . . . ?" (Luke 10:40). Did she really imagine that *He* did not care? She certainly knew better.

Jesus said to Martha, "You are worried and troubled about many things. But one thing is needed, and Mary has chosen that good part" (Luke 10:41–42). This reply must have utterly startled Martha. It didn't seem to have occurred to her that she might be the one in the wrong, but the little scene earned her the gentlest of admonitions from Jesus. Luke's account ends there, so we're probably safe to conclude that the message penetrated straight to Martha's heart.

Indeed, in the later incident recorded in John 12, where Mary anointed Jesus' feet, Martha once again is seen in the role of server. But this time Judas was the one who complained (John 12:4–5). Martha wisely seems to have held her peace this time. She no longer seemed resentful of Mary's devotion to Christ.

As people who love Christ, we must never become so concerned with doing things for Him that we begin to neglect hearing Him and remembering what He has done for us. We must never allow our service for Christ to crowd out our worship of Him. The moment our works become more important to us than our worship, we have lost sight of our true spiritual priorities.

Wasn't Martha simply fulfilling her God-given role of service to the Lord by focusing on the practical matters of hospitality? Give a biblical perspective on what was happening in that situation.

_____

_____

_____

How often do you find yourself sinning even while doing something for the Lord? How do you respond in such circumstances?

_____

_____

_____

Explain how Martha's heart issue here was fundamentally pride. Then look at how graciously Jesus treats her. Examine your own heart, and repent of your own unnoticed or unacknowledged pride, knowing that He will likewise be merciful to you.

_____

_____

_____

Mary Magdalene

*Now the first day of the week Mary
Magdalene went to the tomb early, while
it was still dark, and saw that the stone
had been taken away from the tomb.*

JOHN 20:1

Mary Magdalene is one of the most recognized fig-
ures in the New Testament, and yet Scripture tells us
decidedly little about her. Her name *Magdalene* likely
indicates that she was from the small fishing village of
Magdala, which was situated on the northwest shore of
the Sea of Galilee. She was probably referred to as Mary
Magdalene to differentiate her from the other Marys
connected to Jesus.

When Luke introduces Mary, he calls her "Mary called Magdalene, out of whom had come seven demons" (Luke 8:2). Mary's past was indeed dark, though contrary to many popular novels and films, there is no indication she was a prostitute or that she had participated in any kind of sordid immorality.

Possessed by seven demons, there was nothing any mere man or woman could do for Mary. She was a veritable prisoner of demonic afflictions and in perpetual agony. Demoniacs in Scripture were always friendless, except in rare cases when devoted family members cared for them. They were perpetually restless because of their inability to escape the constant torments of their demonic captors. They were continually joyless because all of life had become darkness and misery for them. And they were hopeless because there was no earthly remedy for their spiritual afflictions.

That is all that can be said with certainty about the past of Mary Magdalene. Scripture deliberately and mercifully omits the macabre details of her dreadful demon possession. But we are given enough information to know that at the very best, she must have been a gloomy, morose, tortured soul. And it is quite likely (especially with so many demons afflicting her) that her case was even worse. She might well have been so demented as to be regarded by most people as an unrecoverable lunatic.

Evil spirits never voluntarily entered the presence of Christ. Nor did they ever knowingly allow one whom they possessed to come close to Him. They often cried against Him (Luke 4:34). They sometimes caused violent convulsions in a last-gasp effort to keep the wretched souls they possessed away from Him (Mark 9:20), but Christ sovereignly drew and delivered multitudes who were possessed by demons (Mark 1:34, 39). Their emancipation from demonic bondage was always instantaneous and complete.

Mary Magdalene was one of them. How and when she was delivered is never spelled out for us, but Christ set her free, and she was free indeed. Having been set free from demons and from sin, she became a slave of righteousness (Romans 6:18). Her life was not merely reformed; it was utterly transformed.

Mary Magdalene joined the close circle of disciples who traveled with Jesus on His long journeys, and she remained His faithful disciple even when others forsook Him. When others became offended with His sayings, she stayed by His side. When others no longer walked with Him, she remained faithful. She followed Him all the way from Galilee to Jerusalem for that final Passover celebration. She ended up loyally following Him to the cross, and even beyond.

Mary Magdalene remained longer than any other disciple at the cross. Then she was the first to reach His tomb at daybreak on the first day of the week. Mary and the women who accompanied her went inside the sepulcher and found it empty. Mary's first inclination was to assume that someone had stolen Jesus' body. Running back the way she came, she encountered Peter and John. She breathlessly told them about the empty tomb, and they both took off running to see for themselves.

> Having been set free from demons and from sin, Mary Magdalene became a slave of righteousness.

A short time later, Mary encountered the risen Jesus. At first, through her tear-filled eyes, she did not recognize Him at all. His countenance was different—glorified. Jesus spoke, "Woman, why are you weeping? Whom are you seeking?" (John 20:15). Mary, thinking He was the gardener, pleaded with Him to show her where they had taken the body of Christ. In response, "Jesus said to her,

'Mary!'" (v. 16). All He had to say was her name, and she instantly recognized Him.

Jesus thus conferred on Mary a unique and unparalleled honor, allowing her to be the first to see and hear Him after His resurrection. That was her extraordinary legacy. No one can ever share that honor or take it from her. But we can, and should, seek to imitate her deep love for Christ.

Your own history of rescue in salvation may not be as dramatic as Mary Magdalene's, but you were no less loosed from bondage to darkness and freed into devotion to Christ than she. How does your life reflect the same gratitude Mary's did?

_____

_____

_____

List the markers in Mary's life of her devotion to God. Could someone do the same for your own life?

_____

_____

_____

Meditate on the honor Christ gave Mary in appearing to her first, after His resurrection. What enabled her to recognize Him at last? How do those facts echo the way any believer comes to recognize the Son of God?

_____

_____

_____

Lydia

Now a certain woman named Lydia
heard us. She was a seller of purple from
the city of Thyatira, who worshiped God.

ACTS 16:14

Lydia is best remembered as the original convert for the gospel in Europe. She was the first person on record ever to respond to the message of Christ during the apostle Paul's original missionary journey into Europe. Ironically, however, Lydia herself was not European. Lydia's hometown was the city of Thyatira, which was in the province of Lydia, her apparent namesake.

Significantly, Thyatira was in the very region of Asia Minor where Luke tells us Paul, Silas, and Timothy "were forbidden by the Holy Spirit to preach the word"

(Acts 16:6). Shortly after all doors were closed to Paul for any further church planting in Asia Minor, God sovereignly led the missionary party into Europe by means of a dream in which a Macedonian man "stood and pleaded with [Paul], saying, 'Come over to Macedonia and help us'" (v. 9).

It was at Philippi in Macedonia that Paul met Lydia. Paul and company spent "some days" in Philippi, apparently waiting for the Sabbath. Paul's normal evangelistic strategy was to take the gospel first to the local synagogue. Philippi, however, was a thoroughly Gentile town with too few Jews for a proper synagogue.

Paul and his group learned the place where Jewish women gathered to pray on the Sabbath, and they went there instead. Luke writes, "On the Sabbath day we went out of the city to the riverside, where prayer was customarily made; and we sat down and spoke to the women who met there" (v. 13). Apparently, the small group of women who gathered there constituted the only public gathering of Jews anywhere in Philippi on a typical Sabbath day. In keeping with his principle of bringing the gospel "[to] the Jew first" (Romans 1:16), Paul went to the riverside to preach.

Ironically, the one woman who responded most

eagerly was not Jewish at all. Lydia was a worshiper of the God of Israel, at least externally. But she was a Gentile, an active seeker of the Lord who had not even yet become a formal Jewish proselyte.

Lydia's faith was immediately evident in her actions. Almost incidentally, Luke said, "And when she and her household were baptized . . ." (Acts 16:15). Remember, the meeting took place next to a river. Apparently, Lydia needed little encouragement to take that first step of obedience to Christ. She was baptized then and there.

Notice also that Scripture mentioned her "household." This could describe her actual family, but nothing in the context indicated she was married. More likely, Lydia was a widow. Her household most likely included servants. She may also have had grown children who lived and traveled with her. But whoever was included in the household, they all came to faith and were baptized right along with Lydia. She was already leading others to Christ. And God was graciously opening their hearts too.

Lydia was also quick to show hospitality to the missionaries. According to Luke, she "begged" them to be her guests: "If you have judged me to be faithful to the Lord, come to my house and stay" (v. 15). Lydia's hospitality to these strangers who had come in the name of

the Lord was commenda-
ble. Again, her eagerness
to host them reminds us
that she was a woman of
means. We know for sure
that the group included
Paul, Silas, Timothy, and
Luke. Likely, there were others. This may have been a
large team. It would be no easy task, even today, to host
so many strangers. Since they had no plans for where to
go next (they were there, after all, to plant a church), she
was offering to keep them indefinitely.

> Lydia's hospitality was as remarkable as her faith—and it is an example for us even today.

Lydia's hospitality was as remarkable as her faith—and
it is an example for us even today. Because of Lydia's generosity to Paul and his missionary team, the gospel obtained
a solid foothold in Philippi. A few short years later, Paul
penned the epistle that bears the name of that church.
It is obvious from the tone of the letter that opposition
to the gospel was still strong in Philippi. But the gospel
was more powerful yet, and from Philippi the testimony
of Christ sounded out into all of Europe. It continues to
spread to the uttermost parts of the earth, even today. But
it all started with the exuberant obedience of one woman,
who offered what she had for the cause of Christ.

List some details that the text of Acts 16 gives to indicate that Lydia's conversion was genuine. What does her conversion have in common with the others we've studied up until now? With your own?

_____

_____

_____

How did Lydia's new faith affect those the Lord had placed immediately around her? How are you finding the same to be true for yourself?

_____

_____

_____

What is so remarkable about Lydia's hospitality— what does it speak to in her character, and what did the Lord use it to accomplish? How are you employing your own resources to similar effect?

_____

_____

_____

Enoch

*Enoch walked with God; and he
was not, for God took him.*

GENESIS 5:24

In all of Scripture there are only a few verses devoted to
the life of Enoch. However, those brief statements are
enough to convey what a remarkable life he lived. They
also provide valuable insights into the love of God and
the calling of faith He has placed upon us.

The first passage containing a reference to Enoch
tells us he "walked with God" (Genesis 5:24). The
term *walk* expresses the idea of moment-by-moment
fellowship with the Lord. And in the early chapters of
Scripture, it is the primary way that someone is identified
as having been forgiven from sin and reconciled to God.

Because Noah walked with God, he escaped judgment (6:9). Because Abraham walked with God, he received blessing (17:1). Because Enoch walked with God, he avoided death.

That kind of fellowship is what God both desires and provides. It is that same kind of relationship that He still offers sinners today. As Jesus told the multitudes to whom He preached, "Come to Me, all you who labor and are heavy laden, and I will give you rest. Take My yoke upon you and learn from Me, for I am gentle and lowly in heart, and you will find rest for your souls" (Matthew 11:28–29). Even now, the Lord is looking for those who will come to Him for forgiveness—based on His substitutionary sacrifice—and walk with Him in fellowship.

As it is with all who walk with God, Enoch's relationship with God was based on faith. The author of Hebrews tells us as much: "Before [Enoch] was taken he had this testimony, that he pleased God. But without faith it is impossible to please Him, for he who comes to God must believe that He is, and that He is a rewarder of those who diligently seek Him" (Hebrews 11:5–6).

Because of His infinite love, God is a lavish rewarder of those who put their faith in Him. He grants sinners forgiveness, clothes them in His righteousness, and creates in them a new heart. God turns former rebels into His children, giving them His Spirit, His blessings, and the promise of eternal life. He has provided the only way for unworthy sinners to have fellowship with Him through His Son Jesus Christ (John 14:6); and of all who come, He will turn none away.

Enoch's walk with the Lord was marked by steadfast faith in the true God. He put his confidence in God's gracious forgiveness and imputed righteousness, knowing that his hope in the Lord would not be disappointed. Faith is the substance of the redeemed life. It was for Enoch, and it must be for us as well.

> Because of His infinite love, God is a lavish rewarder of those who put their faith in Him.

Like any godly person would be, Enoch was deeply disturbed over the spiritual ruin of the souls in his society. And he took action to warn them about God's impending judgment. Genesis 5:21 indicates that Enoch named his son "Methuselah"—a name that means either "man of the javelin" or "man of the sending forth." Evidently, the Lord had revealed to Enoch that judgment would be suddenly unleashed on the earth (sent forth like a javelin), but that it would not come until after Methuselah died. Thus, even the name of Enoch's son was a warning to the world of his day.

Enoch was sixty-five years old when Methuselah was born. According to Genesis 5:22, it was at that point in his life when Enoch really began to walk with God. Perhaps this was due to the realization that divine judgment was imminent. But whatever the cause, from that event on, he diligently sought the Lord, and he also sought salvation for the people around him. Enoch faithfully warned the world about the coming wrath of God. Even though he would never see that judgment himself, Enoch boldly proclaimed it, nonetheless.

The Genesis account of Enoch's life draws the final curtain by stating simply, "He was not, for God took him" (5:24). Enoch vanished from this earth without a trace. He took a walk with God and never came back. Of course, Enoch's walk with God did not end when he stepped into heaven. Rather, it was perfected. Though we may not escape death in this life, we possess the same hope Enoch had. As those who have put our faith in Jesus Christ, walking with Him in full forgiveness and intimate fellowship, we can rest assured that we have escaped eternal death and will live instead in perfect eternal life.

The earliest chapters of the Bible give rich meaning to the concept of walking with the Lord. Fill out that picture to explain it explicitly by referencing the New Testament (e.g., John 8:12; Romans 6:1–4; Ephesians 4:1ff.; Philippians 3:15–17; Colossians 2:6ff.).

_____

_____

_____

What does Hebrews 11:5–6 reveal was the basis of Enoch's intimacy with the true and living God? What does that tell you about how God has always saved His chosen people?

_____

_____

_____

Explain how faith is the substance of the redeemed life.

_____

_____

_____

Joseph

But as for you, you meant evil against me; but God meant it for good, in order to bring it about as it is this day, to save many people alive.

GENESIS 50:20

Young Joseph was his father's favorite son. Not only did he have Jacob's favor and affection, he was also given a special coat—a royal robe fitted to his special position— and a place of authority over his brothers. But Joseph's favored status wasn't free from its challenges. It aroused jealousy within his brothers, and he became the object of their contempt and scorn.

It probably didn't help that Joseph was a dreamer. His accounts of seemingly outrageous dreams, in which his brothers paid homage to him, did nothing to quell their rage. After one dream, Joseph reported, "Look, I have dreamed another dream. And this time, the sun, the moon, and the eleven stars bowed down to me" (Genesis 37:9). Though the Bible never attributes sinful pride to Joseph even in sharing his dreams, the dreams fed his brothers' hatred of him. They began seeking the opportunity to divest the dreamer of both his royal robe and his place in the family.

One day, far from home, the opportunity came knocking. The brothers were tending the family's flocks when they saw Joseph coming up the road on his way to check up on them. Quickly, they devised a plan. They grabbed him, stripped him of his special robe, and dumped him into a dry well. Scared and confused, Joseph must have cried for help inside his dark prison, but his brothers paid no attention.

Judah suggested they sell Joseph into slavery. Shortly thereafter, the terrified teenager was hoisted out of the cistern and handed over to a group of North Arabian traders headed for Egypt. Joseph had descended from being the favored son to being a kidnapped slave. Surely, he wondered why God permitted this to happen and how this fit with the dreams God had given him.

Once in Egypt, Joseph was sold as a slave to Potiphar, a chief servant of the pharaoh. However, he quickly rose to a position of prominence in Potiphar's house. While there, Joseph was introduced to royalty and the noble customs of Egypt. Such knowledge would later prove essential. This placement in Potiphar's home also ensured that, if he were ever found guilty of a crime, he would be sent to the same place where the pharaoh's own prisoners were confined.

Before long, Joseph *was* accused of a terrible crime. Driven by her own lustful desires, Potiphar's wife repeatedly attempted to seduce Joseph, and he repeatedly rejected her every attempt. One day, scorned by his refusals, she accused Joseph of attempted rape. Joseph was sent to prison.

> Joseph woke up in a prison cell one morning, and by that evening, he had become, next to the pharaoh, the most powerful ruler in the land.

It sounds strange, but even in prison Joseph experienced the Lord's blessing. Not only were his administrative skills noticed by the warden, who soon placed Joseph in charge of all prison operations, but he was also able to catch the attention of the pharaoh.

One night the pharaoh awoke, startled by the most vivid and terrible nightmare—seven skinny cows devouring seven fat cows, then seven withered heads of grain gobbling up seven plump heads. The next day, the pharaoh was deeply troubled, and even more so when none of his wise men could tell him what the dream meant. It was then that the royal cupbearer, who had been in prison years earlier, remembered that Joseph had once interpreted a dream for him.

Without delay, the pharaoh sent for Joseph, and Joseph explained that the dream was a warning: seven years of bountiful harvests would be followed by seven years of devastating famine. If the Egyptians were to be ready for the coming catastrophe, they would have to begin storing up resources immediately. Moreover, a man with administrative skill would be needed to organize the collection and storage effort. Of course, Joseph was that man. That morning, Joseph woke up in a prison cell. By evening, he had become, next to the pharaoh, the most powerful ruler in the land.

It was in this position that Joseph came face-to-face with his brothers once again. But rather than lashing out in vengeance, he forgave them, embraced them, and saved their lives. Why? Because Joseph understood that despite their evil actions, it was really God who had been writing his story all along.

The Lord is writing our stories too. Even when others hurt us or life seems difficult and unfair, we can triumphantly declare with Joseph, "As for you, you meant evil against me; but God meant it for good" (50:20).

Joseph's life exhibits an almost unrivaled faith in God's sovereignty. Do you struggle to trust God's revelation, rather than your circumstances, to order and interpret your life? How in this area can you be more like Joseph?

_____

_____

_____

Would you have successfully resisted the temptation for revenge against the brothers who sold you into slavery? Why or why not? What enabled Joseph to do just that?

_____

_____

_____

How differently would you have lived in the past if you'd believed that God sovereignly ordained every twist and turn of your life? How can you begin living like that now?

_____

_____

_____

Miriam

Then Miriam the prophet, Aaron's sister, took a timbrel in her hand, and all the women followed her, with timbrels and dancing.

EXODUS 15:20

As a young girl and the daughter of slaves, Miriam was certainly an unlikely hero. Yet she played a vital role in the life of her baby brother, Moses, at a critical time in his young life—when he was only three months old. We don't know exactly how old Miriam was at the time, yet God used her in a crucial way to accomplish His perfect purposes for her brother—and ultimately for the nation of Israel.

Their mother, Jochebed, had placed Moses in a basket lined with waterproof pitch and set him adrift on the Nile River. The pharaoh had ordered all Hebrew baby boys to be murdered by drowning, but Jochebed and her husband, Amram, had hidden baby Moses for three months, refusing to obey the pharaoh's cruel edict and believing God had a special purpose for their boy. When they could hide him no longer, Jochebed carefully placed her son in the river and into the hands of God.

Miriam followed the basket and watched as her baby brother was discovered by none other than the daughter of the pharaoh. Miriam closed the safe distance between herself and royalty. She bravely approached the pharaoh's daughter without identifying herself and suggested that perhaps a Hebrew nursemaid might have some success in comforting the baby. In a shrewd and bold action, she asked, "Shall I go and call a nurse for you from the Hebrew women, that she may nurse the child for you?" (Exodus 2:7). The princess agreed, and Miriam's strategy unfolded as she went to find her mother.

God's providence brought about a remarkable result. Miriam's courage led to Moses' mother being paid to raise her own son! She could do so at home, and without any fear of the Egyptian authorities.

It is likely that Moses lived with his birth family until he was nine or ten years old, and maybe even until he was twelve. When the day came for Moses to leave for the palace, Miriam was no doubt there to say goodbye. As she watched him leave, she would surely have wondered when God would elevate Moses to deliver her enslaved people from Egypt.

But she would have to wait many long decades. When Moses was forty years old, he murdered an Egyptian in a futile attempt to be a savior to his people. That mistake cost him his position in the pharaoh's court, and he was forced to flee Egypt. Another forty years passed while Moses tended sheep in Midian and started a family. Finally, when Moses was eighty years old, he had his encounter with God at the burning bush and received the call to return to Egypt to deliver God's people.

> Miriam's greatest triumphs came when her heart was centered on the glory of God.

Undoubtedly, Miriam's excitement grew when Moses and their brother, Aaron, first confronted the pharaoh and then with each successive plague. As frogs, flies, lice, boils, hail, and locusts afflicted the Egyptians, Miriam and her fellow Hebrews— protected by God in Goshen—must have been filled with awe and a growing realization that the Lord had finally heard their cries (Exodus 3:7). Their redemption from bondage was at hand.

Miriam and her family participated in the first Passover. They killed a lamb and painted its blood on the doorposts of their house. They were kept safe as God's judgment was handed out in the slaughter of all the first-born sons of Egypt. It is not difficult to imagine her relief as she was awakened early that next morning with the news that it was time to leave.

Later, on the shore of the Red Sea, we get a glimpse into the heart of the woman that Miriam had become. After experiencing the miraculous parting of the water and the destruction of the pharaoh's army, she led the women of Israel in song: "Sing to the LORD, for He has triumphed gloriously! The horse and its rider He has thrown into the sea!" (15:21).

Miriam is rightly worthy of our admiration, not because of her own greatness, but because she rested in faith on the mighty power of God. In that, there is an example for us to follow. Though Miriam's life was notable on many fronts, her greatest triumphs came when her heart was centered on the glory of God. Let us choose to do the same—to let every circumstance that comes our way remind us that God is always faithful and worthy of our praise.

Though only a young girl in Exodus 2, Miriam was pivotal to God's plan of deliverance for His people. How else have you seen God use the humble and overlooked things to forward His plan of redemption?

_____

_____

_____

When have you had to wait long periods, even decades of suffering, for the fruition of your hopes? Contemplate Miriam and all Israel's experience in Egypt; how does Scripture tell you to interpret how the Lord is working here?

_____

_____

_____

In the face of the tragedies visited on the Egyptians, why is Miriam's leading public exultation, as recorded in Exodus 15, laudable?

_____

_____

_____

Gideon

And the Angel of the LORD appeared
to him, and said to him, "The LORD is
with you, you mighty man of valor!"

JUDGES 6:12

If you were looking for a military commander to take on an impossible mission, you'd probably look for someone with tremendous courage, a track record of performing well under pressure—perhaps someone with an intimidating presence too. Gideon had none of these qualities, and yet he was handpicked by God to deliver His people from the cruel and formidable Midianite army.

Gideon's life is an example of the strength of God being displayed in weakness (see 2 Corinthians 12:9). When we first meet Gideon, this weakness is evident:

he is hiding from the Midianites—attempting to thresh wheat covertly in a winepress (Judges 6:11). The process of beating out grain and separating it from the chaff normally took place out in the open, on a hilltop, where the breeze would blow away the chaff. But fearful that enemy marauders might spot him, Gideon took cover in the quarried shelter of a winepress. No one would have accused Gideon of being overly courageous.

Gideon also struggled to muster the faith necessary to trust God's promises. Even though the angel of the Lord had promised Gideon victory in his campaign against the Midianites, Gideon wasn't convinced he was the right man for the job. In his doubt, he asked God for a miraculous sign: he left a fleece of wool on the threshing floor and asked the Lord to soak it with dew while keeping the ground around it dry. But when God gave Gideon the very sign he asked for, he asked for another. This time, he wanted the ground to be wet and the fleece to be bone dry. God, in His great patience, gave Gideon what his trembling heart needed.

> The Lord met Gideon in his weakness.

Of course, Gideon's actions should not be viewed as a pattern for believers to follow. As Christians, we do not ascertain the validity of God's Word by asking Him for miraculous confirmation. Instead, we live according to His will by believing Him and being obedient to His Word. Even though God's promise should have been enough for Gideon, the Lord still met him in his weakness.

Neither Gideon's lack of courage nor his timid faith disqualified him from his assignment. In fact, when Gideon had assembled a volunteer army of thirty-two thousand capable Israelites—still a small army compared to the military might of Midian—the Lord commanded him to downsize. He wanted Israel to know it was His power, not theirs, that brought their deliverance (7:2). Gideon had been nervous with an army of thirty-two thousand, so imagine how he felt when twenty-two thousand of those men packed up and left for home.

Ten thousand warriors remained, but God wasn't finished slimming down Israel's forces. He had Gideon lead the army to a nearby brook. Every man who cupped the water and lapped it up like a dog could stay, while every man who got down on his knees to drink was sent home. In the end, only three hundred men remained.

From the standpoint of proven military tactics, reducing one's army from thirty-two thousand to three hundred makes no sense. But the Lord was declaring an unmistakable point—not just for Gideon but for all of Israel and for us. They were about to see His power put on display; it was time for them to be courageous, not because they themselves were strong, but because the Lord fought on their behalf.

In the dark of night, Gideon's army blew trumpets, smashed pitchers, held up blazing torches, and shouted, "The sword of the LORD and of Gideon!" (v. 20). Dazed and disoriented, the half-asleep Midianites panicked. Thinking there must be Israelite soldiers everywhere in their camp, the Midianites were unable to distinguish friend from enemy, and slashed a path of escape through one another.

Incredibly, the Lord used Gideon, a faint-hearted grain farmer, to deliver His people from their deadly enemies. He was the most unlikely of potential heroes, but God elevated him to win a decisive battle against impossible odds—not to exalt Gideon but to demonstrate His mighty power to save His people. In response, Gideon rightly recognized that the Lord alone deserved all the glory.

Despite his palpable fear and weak faith, Gideon did all that the Lord asked of him. In that, he proved himself a worthy servant. His example of faith-filled dependence on the Lord serves as a perpetual reminder that God supplies strength to those who trust in Him.

Summarize Gideon's character. Why does he still merit mention in Hebrews 11?

_____

_____

_____

Recall specific instances when God was gracious to you despite your own weak faith, and praise Him for His goodness.

_____

_____

_____

Consider how far the Lord went to demonstrate to His people why, against incredible odds, they should be courageous. Have you taken this lesson to heart better than Israel did? Why or why not?

_____

_____

_____

Samson

*Then Samson called to the
Lord, saying, "O Lord God,
remember me, I pray!"*

JUDGES 16:28

Samson, one of Israel's judges prior to the monarchy, is
something of a walking contradiction. He was a man
endowed with supernatural strength whose feats of might
belong to the world of children's fantasy heroes. Yet that
unparalleled strength and power, corrupted and forfeited
by his untamed passion, diminished him into a tragically
pitiful weakling. But when he was weakest, the Lord used
Samson in the mightiest act of his astonishing life.

Before he was even born, God set Samson apart to
deliver Israel from the hand of the wicked Philistines.

The angel of the Lord visited Samson's parents and promised his barren mother that she would know the joy of holding a baby son in her arms. The Lord told her Samson was to be a Nazirite. In Numbers 6:1–8, the Lord gave specific restrictions for those who took this vow of separation: no drinking of alcohol, no cutting of the hair, and no touching of a dead body. This was to symbolize the person's commitment to holy living.

The fact that Samson from birth was to be separated had little effect on how he lived as an adult. He became a man driven by fleshly desires, especially his unrestrained passion

> Samson's wild disregard for the Lord's clear commands made his life a legendary tragedy.

for pagan women. Scripture describes him as having a stubborn will, irrational desires, and a violent temper—a volatile combination. Ultimately, Samson's wild disregard for the Lord's clear commands would make his life a legendary tragedy, with his infatuation for Philistine women at the center.

If Samson were Superman, his own sinful desires were his kryptonite. He could kill a lion, but not his lust. He could break new ropes, but not old habits. He could defeat armies of Philistine soldiers, but not his own flesh. He could carry away the gates of a city but allowed himself to be carried away when lost in passion.

Though he is identified as one of his nation's foremost judges, Samson never made any attempt to drive Israel's enemies out of the land. In fact, he was happy to interact with the Philistines, even to the point of marrying one of them. Though he was only interested in serving himself, the Lord would superintend Samson's selfish choices to secure Israel's deliverance and ensure Philistia's demise (cf. Judges 14:4).

Never is this more clearly visible than with Samson's lustful relationship with the Philistine Delilah. Knowing that Delilah had Samson's attention, the leaders of the Philistines bribed her to discover the secret of Samson's strength. With a fortune at stake, Delilah was more than happy to seduce her Hebrew boyfriend. She pleaded, and she manipulated, and she eventually wore him down. He told her, "If I am shaven, then my strength will leave me, and I shall become weak, and be like any other man" (16:17).

Delilah wasted no time. She coaxed Samson to sleep and called for a local barber. When the Philistine guards arrived to apprehend him, Samson was helpless.

Never before had he been unable to overpower all enemies; never again would he escape from their custody. Samson, so long blinded by might, arrogance, and lust, was now blinded by his captors, who gouged out his eyes and put him to work as a grinder in the prison at Gaza.

The Philistines gave the credit for Samson's defeat to their god, Dagon, for whom they held a great celebration. Utterly debased, Samson was led into the idol's temple. He then asked for what seemed like a small courtesy to such a wretched figure—to be led between the central pillars so that he could steady himself by leaning on them.

Samson, unable to see, knew he was right where he needed to be. In one final prayer, he asked the Lord to give him back his strength for a climactic, self-sacrificing, heroic act. With a mighty push and a catastrophic crash, the entire structure collapsed, crushing everyone inside it. Samson's valor shows that, in the humiliation and brokenness of his last days, he had come to truly depend on the Lord. He became a hero of faith by trusting God to use him in death and bring him into His presence.

Most of Samson's life serves as an example of how *not* to live, but in his death there is a powerful lesson not to be missed: Spiritual victory comes by way of humility, by recognizing that God is the only true power. It is when we are weak that He shows Himself strongest.

In what ways was Samson mighty? In what ways was he feeble? Frankly assess your own life along the same lines.

_____

_____

_____

Does Samson's narrative condone his disdainful disregard for the Lord's clear commands? Why or why not?

_____

_____

_____

Why, despite its obvious tragic elements, is Samson's story not merely a tragedy? Who is its true hero?

_____

_____

_____

Jonathan

You shall be king over Israel,
and I shall be next to you. Even
my father Saul knows that.

1 SAMUEL 23:17

Though Jonathan was the son of Saul, Israel's first king, he was nothing like his father. Where Saul was faithless and timid, Jonathan trusted the Lord with boldness. This is perhaps no more clearly seen than in back-to-back accounts of father and son preserved for us in 1 Samuel 13–14.

During a conflict with the Philistines, Samuel gave Saul instructions to wait for him at Gilgal. In seven days, Samuel would offer a sacrifice there on the altar, and the Lord would deliver the Philistines into Saul's hands. But the Philistines were fierce, and many of Saul's men went into hiding. Saul, who was no stranger to fear, was filled with dread. When Samuel failed to arrive within the seven-day timeframe, Saul decided to take matters into his own hands and offer the sacrifice himself.

As soon as Saul had finished presenting the burnt offering, Samuel arrived, surveyed the scene, and lamented, "What have you done?" (1 Samuel 13:11). As a result of Saul's disobedience, Samuel announced, "You have not kept the commandment of the LORD your God, which He commanded you. For now the LORD would have established your kingdom over Israel forever. But now your kingdom shall not continue" (vv. 13–14).

Meanwhile, Jonathan and his armor-bearer left to take on a Philistine garrison. To reach it, the pair would have to freeclimb up the face of a craggy cliff characterized by slippery rocks and sharp thistles. Then, they would need to subdue a mob of angry Philistines by themselves. Many would have seen such an operation as a suicide mission, but not Jonathan. Turning to his armor-bearer, he said, "Come, let us go over to the garrison of these uncircumcised; it may be that the LORD will work for us. For nothing restrains the LORD from saving by many or by few" (14:6). Jonathan was fearless—not because he was confident in his own ability, but because he had placed his faith firmly in the promised will and power of God. If the Lord fought for them, the two of them would be enough.

The Lord gave Jonathan and his armor-bearer more power than twenty heavily armed soldiers (see 1 Samuel 13:19–23). When the Philistine army heard this, they were full of fear and began to scatter. God struck further terror in their hearts by causing an earthquake that sent them into a confused panic so that they began to kill one another. Jonathan had been exactly right: nothing restrains the Lord from saving by many or by few. His faith secured the victory, while his father's faithlessness forfeited the throne.

Of course, the throne would have likely passed to Jonathan if God had not rejected Saul. For this reason, Jonathan's love for David, the man God chose to succeed his father, tells us much about Jonathan's faithfulness to the Lord. Jonathan willingly gave up his own claim to the throne because he understood that God had chosen David instead of him. And he had no resentment, only affection for the one who would reign in his

> Jonathan willingly gave up his own claim to the throne because he understood that God had chosen David instead of him.

place. Ironically, while Saul tenaciously (and futilely) tried to retain the throne for his son, his son happily offered it to the man he knew was God's choice to be Israel's ruler. Jonathan did not merely accept his non-kingly role; he embraced it wholeheartedly—eagerly protecting and promoting the one whom God had appointed to be king instead of him.

Even though Jonathan died in battle, his legacy lived on because of his special friendship with David. Years earlier, the two men had sworn an oath to each other: "May the LORD be between you and me, and between your descendants and my descendants, forever" (1 Samuel 20:42). David honored that vow when he became king by seeking out Mephibosheth—Jonathan's sole descendant—and inviting him to the palace where he was welcomed like one of David's own sons. David further gave Mephibosheth the land that had previously belonged to his grandfather, Saul, and instructed Saul's former servants to continue working the land for their master's grandson.

Jesus said, "Greater love has no one than this, than to lay down one's life for his friends" (John 15:13). In Jonathan, we have a vibrant example of a man who laid down his life while he was still living—gladly giving up all personal honor, power, and position for a friend because it was the will of God that he should do so.

Why was Jonathan's raid on the Philistine garrison not foolhardiness, but faith? How do you know that is true from the text?

_____

_____

_____

_____

Scripture's narrative indicates that Jonathan could have served Israel as a valorous, wise, and faithful king. Reflect on his humble submission to the Lord's plan.

_____

_____

_____

_____

Do you think you could have embraced God's plan with as much joy and loyalty as Jonathan did, given all that was on the line? When have you faced such tests of faith in your own life, and how have you succeeded or failed?

_____

_____

_____

_____

31

Jonah

But Jonah arose to flee to Tarshish
from the presence of the LORD.

JONAH 1:3

Jonah was asleep in the hold of the ship as the Gentile
sailors scurried about above, bailing water and tossing any
unnecessary cargo overboard. The boat may have been
heaving and the crew may have been overwrought, but,
incredibly, Jonah was not. It was only the ship's captain
waking him that brought Jonah to conscious awareness
of the chaos and deadly danger of the storm.

Once awake, however, Jonah quickly realized the
great risk he'd taken boarding the ship. When the crew
cast lots to find who was to blame for angering the
gods, Jonah was singled out and his suspicions were

confirmed—he was God's target in the tempest. A short time earlier, perhaps only a few weeks or even days, the Lord had come to Jonah with a simple command, "Arise, go to Nineveh, that great city, and cry out against it; for their wickedness has come up before Me" (Jonah 1:2). The mandate was clear and direct: preach a message of repentance or judgment to the Assyrians in their capital city of Nineveh.

For Jonah, however, that directive seemed unreasonable—and the thought of submitting to it was utterly distasteful. He knew that Nineveh was as wicked as it was impressive. Assyrian kings boasted of the horrific ways in which they massacred their enemies and mutilated their captives. They posed a clear and present danger to the national security of Israel, where Jonah ministered as a prophet. To take a message of repentance and hope to Israel's hated pagan enemies was unthinkable. So Jonah decided to disobey the Lord's command and travel as far as he could in the opposite direction.

But spiritual rebellion reaps what it sows, as God reproves and corrects those whom He loves (Hebrews 12:6). In Jonah's case, that correction came swiftly and dramatically, as his Tarshish-bound vessel was suddenly engulfed by a furious storm. The recalcitrant missionary instructed the frightened sailors, "Pick me up and throw me into the sea; then the sea will become calm for you. For I know that this great tempest is because of me" (Jonah 1:12). In effect, Jonah was saying he would rather die than fulfill his mission to the Ninevites.

The supernatural character of the raging storm became immediately apparent as soon as Jonah hit the water—the wind instantly stopped and the massive waves flattened. Jonah was gone, and so was the storm. But the Lord was not done with him yet. Rather than allowing him to drown, "the LORD had prepared a great fish to swallow Jonah. And Jonah was in the belly of the fish three days and three nights" (v. 17).

> Jonah recoiled at the thought of God extending mercy to Assyria and then begged the Lord for grace and compassion from the depths of his own desperation.

Amid this misery, the humbled prophet cried out for deliverance. The man who recoiled at the thought of God extending mercy to Assyria begged the Lord for grace and compassion from the depths of his own desperation. God graciously answered his prayer. Three days later, a wet, disheveled, slime-covered prophet collapsed with a stench onto the sandy beach. He had just been violently expelled from his gastric prison by a fish that had endured three days of indigestion so the Lord could teach Jonah a lesson.

Jonah's message in Nineveh was little more than a threat: "Yet forty days, and Nineveh shall be overthrown!" (3:4). What happened next was a far more extreme and amazing miracle than the prophet-swallowing fish had been: "the people of Nineveh believed God" (v. 5). Those few words describe the largest-scale revival recorded in the Old Testament, as the entire population of Nineveh—numbering more than 120,000—repented and turned to the Lord.

While most missionaries would be delighted with such a harvest, Jonah was not. He recognized the magnitude of God's grace and wanted nothing to do with the divine pardon being extended to Israel's hostile enemies. The book ends abruptly with Jonah still sulking over the Lord's generous mercy.

Like Jonah, we might be tempted to allow our own fears, prejudices, or selfish interests to inhibit our gospel witness. But when we prioritize the gospel message over our own personal agendas, we bring glory to God as we advance His kingdom purposes throughout the world.

Give examples from the text that demonstrate Jonah's attitude toward God. Considering the same record and Hebrews 12:6, what can we conclude about God's attitude toward Jonah?

_____

_____

_____

What is the through line of Jonah's story—what do we learn about man's nature versus God's nature?

_____

_____

_____

What does the book of Jonah tell us about how God chooses to advance the gospel?

_____

_____

_____

Esther

Yet who knows whether you have come
to the kingdom for such a time as this?

ESTHER 4:14

There were approximately 25 million women living in
the Persian Empire when Ahasuerus began his search
for a new queen. Only four hundred young women were
selected. Esther, a young Jewish orphan girl in the city
of Susa, was among them.

There was a year of beautification and primping
leading to the final preparation when a virgin would go
before the emperor, looking as pretty as possible and,
with the aid of incense and cosmetic burners, smelling
unforgettable. In the end, twelve months of intensive
preparation came down to one opportunity to impress

the king. For that all-important encounter, each young lady was allowed to adorn herself with whatever apparel or jewelry she desired. The day after being presented to the ruler, she would join the other concubines in another part of the palace, where she would wait indefinitely, hoping the king would choose her.

Like an ancient Cinderella story, when it was Esther's turn, she stole the king's heart and became his queen. Thus, an obscure Jewish orphan girl was exalted to the highest position of any woman in the world at that time. Out of all the women in the empire, it had come down to Esther being singled out by the king himself. This was clearly no coincidence. A power infinitely greater than Ahasuerus was at work, orchestrating His purposes through the emperor's affections.

Significantly, throughout the entire process, Esther kept her Jewish identity a secret—just as her cousin Mordecai instructed her to do. This was likely due to the strong anti-Semitism that existed in the Persian Empire at that time (cf. Ezra 4:6). Esther would reveal her ethnic heritage, but not until the situation left her with no option.

In the third chapter of Esther, we are introduced to the villain Haman, a man whom the king had exalted above his other princes and royal officials. We are reminded that Haman was an Agagite, a descendent of the Amalekite King Agag. Four centuries earlier, God had ordered Saul to kill Agag; but he disobeyed and let Agag live. The prophet Samuel later executed God's command and hacked Agag to death (1 Samuel 15:32–33).

Haman carried feelings of intense hatred toward the Israelites because of this history, and so he went to the king and proposed that all Jews living within the Persian Empire be killed. Trusting his chief courtier and falsely thinking he was going to squelch a rebellion before it began, Ahasuerus authorized genocide.

Before long, Mordecai informed Esther of what Haman had done and urged her to plead with the king on behalf of the lives of the Jews. Mordecai's plan for Esther's appeal sounded simple enough. But in Persia, no one, including the queen, could appear before the king without his express invitation.

The queen was understandably afraid of her potentially violent and irrational husband. But Mordecai urged her to be courageous: "If you remain completely silent at this time, relief and deliverance will arise for the Jews from another place, but you and your father's house will perish. Yet who knows whether you have come to the kingdom for such a time as this?" (Esther 4:13–14).

Embracing her divinely granted role, Esther approached the throne tensely, wondering what the king's response would be; the seconds felt like hours as she waited for Ahasuerus to acknowledge her presence. Then it happened: he looked at her and extended his royal scepter to her, eagerly welcoming her beauty into his presence.

Esther's willingness to use her position in service to God's people triggered a series of events in which Haman's wicked plot was finally uncovered. In the end, Ahasuerus overrode the order to exterminate the Jewish people from the empire and ordered Haman sent to the gallows. The king later exalted Mordecai to second-in-command over the entire empire.

The real hero in this story is never mentioned, never even named, but God Himself is the only explanation for the survival of the Jews amid such hatred and

> The real hero in this story is never mentioned, never even named—but God Himself is the only explanation for the survival of the Jews amid such hatred and opposition.

opposition. His hand of providence is in every large event and every small detail as He protects and preserves His people.

God's sovereign plan will prevail; there is no stopping it. But like Esther before us, we must choose whether we will act as willing instruments in His hands for the good of the world. Wherever you may live, you are there for such a time as this.

How was Mordecai's famous statement in Esther 4:13–14 a true expression of faith versus merely a threat or wishful thinking (cf. Isa. 11:11–12)?

_____

_____

_____

_____

How do you tend to see the privileges God has given you as primarily for your own benefit? How can you be more purposeful about using them in service of God's people and purposes?

_____

_____

_____

Reflect on your own situation, however humble or exalted. Identify at least three ways you can uniquely honor God's sovereignty in it by being bold for His glory.

_____

_____

_____

John the Baptist

*Assuredly, I say to you, among those
born of women there has not risen one
greater than John the Baptist.*

MATTHEW 11:11

Using any set of worldly criteria for greatness, John the
Baptist would not be deemed great. He was not born into
a wealthy or powerful family. His parents, Zacharias and
Elizabeth, were both from the priestly tribe of Levi. But
there were many Levites in Israel at the time—so many
that John's family did not have any special social status.

While still a teenager, John abandoned the comforts
and conveniences of civilized society and moved to the
Judean wilderness, becoming a hermit-like, homeless
preacher. According to Matthew 3:4, "John himself was

clothed in camel's hair, with a leather belt around his waist; and his food was locusts and wild honey." Nothing about his lineage, his contrary social behavior, his external appearance, or his diet suggested that he should be considered anything but odd.

John was cut off from formal education, living in isolation in the desert. He instigated no permanent social, political, or religious movement. Though the populace was drawn to his message of the Messiah's arrival, the authorities (such as the Pharisees and scribes) resented him fiercely. Only a small band of disciples continued to follow him—and then, only briefly. His ministry was relatively short; he died ignominiously at the hands of a petty ruler. Nothing in his life fit the model associated with greatness.

> Nothing about John's lineage, his contrary social behavior, his external appearance, or his diet suggested that he should be considered anything but odd.

Despite all that, John was what the angel Gabriel said he would be: "great in the sight of the Lord" (Luke 1:15). Incredibly, the Lord not only declared him to be a great man, but the greatest man who had ever lived. That declaration came from the lips of Jesus Christ Himself: "Assuredly, I say to you, among those born of women there has not risen one greater than John the Baptist" (Matthew 11:11).

John lived much of his life in the obscurity of the Judean desert before the word of God came to him, initiating his prophetic ministry when he was about thirty years old (Luke 3:2). At that time, he suddenly "came baptizing in the wilderness and preaching a baptism of repentance for the remission of sins" (Mark 1:4).

John was a contrast in every respect—from his prolonged isolation to his abrupt public appearance, from his rugged wilderness life to his dramatic preaching and baptizing ministry. He was born to a woman who could not have children. He came from a line of priests but ministered as a prophet. And he reached Jewish society by removing himself from it.

In Matthew 11:9, Jesus separated John from the noble prophets before him by saying he was "more than a prophet" because—as the Lord went on to explain—he was the divinely appointed messenger foretold in Malachi 3:1. John's mission had been prophesied some seven hundred years earlier by Isaiah: "The voice of one crying in the wilderness: 'Prepare the way of the Lord; make His paths straight'" (Matthew 3:3; cf. Isaiah 40:3–4). He was preparing the hearts of the Jews for the coming of their long-awaited King. After millennia of anticipation and prophetic promises, John was selected for the unparalleled privilege of being the Messiah's personal herald.

Not diminishing any of John's greatness, given his special role in the plan of redemption, Jesus made the surprising statement: "he who is least in the kingdom of heaven is greater than [John]" (Matthew 11:11). In saying that, Jesus was emphasizing the spiritual privilege that all New Testament believers enjoy. John was greater than the Old Testament prophets because he personally participated in the fulfillment of what they had merely anticipated from a distance (cf. 1 Peter 1:10–11). But all believers after the cross and resurrection enjoy even greater privilege still because we participate in the full understanding and experience of something John only anticipated—the actual atoning work of Christ.

Upon arriving in heaven, our privilege will be elevated infinitely, as was John's. There, our faith will be sight and our hope will be realized as we praise our Savior face to face. John's unique greatness was about his role in human history. In terms of spiritual inheritance, however, even John's earthly greatness cannot compare to what he and every believer will enjoy in the glories of heaven—not because of anything within themselves but because of the all-surpassing greatness of Jesus Christ.

John the Baptist exhibited none of the usual markers of greatness. Can you explain the Lord's statement about him in the first half of Matthew 11:11?

_____

_____

_____

What made John "more than a prophet" (Matt. 11:9)?

_____

_____

_____

Especially given the above considerations, how can we make sense of the conclusion of Jesus' statement in Matthew 11:11, that "he who is least in the kingdom of heaven is greater than [John]"? What kind of greatness does God care about?

_____

_____

_____

James, the Brother of Our Lord

And after they had become silent,
James answered, saying, "Men
and brethren, listen to me."

ACTS 15:13

Can you imagine what it must have been like to grow up in the same family as Jesus? For the brothers and sisters of our Lord, there was no imagining; it was their daily reality. The Bible tells us that Jesus was part of a large family. He was, of course, Mary's oldest child. But after He was born, Mary and Joseph had four more sons and at least two daughters (Matthew 13:55–56; Mark 6:3).

No indication is given in any of the four Gospels that Jesus' brothers came to believe in Him during the years of His public ministry. To the contrary, we're told they believed Jesus to be "out of His mind" (Mark 3:21; cf. John 7:5). But after His death, resurrection, and ascension, there was a dramatic and miraculous change. His brothers were present among the believers who gathered in the upper room, awaiting the coming of the Spirit at Pentecost.

According to Acts 1:14, after Jesus ascended to heaven, the apostles "continued with one accord in prayer and supplication, with the women and Mary the mother of Jesus, and with His brothers." No longer antagonistic, Jesus' brothers had come to believe in Him as Messiah and Lord. What had produced this miracle? How had His recalcitrant brothers—James in particular—come to saving faith, joining the ranks of Jesus' followers?

The amazing answer is found in 1 Corinthians 15, where Paul surveyed the post-resurrection appearances of our Lord. In the list, he included this detail: "He was seen by James" (v. 7). Jesus personally appeared after His resurrection to James. What a stunning reunion that must have been! Undoubtedly, it was the moment of

James's conversion and explains why he was among the believers in the upper room. He had seen the resurrected Christ and confessed his brother as Lord.

So James—the stubbornly skeptical second-born son of Mary—came all the way to saving faith in his older half-brother, the Lord Jesus Christ, through a post-resurrection appearance. Although he had known Jesus for more than three decades, he did not believe in Him until his risen brother graciously appeared to him and saved him. At the establishment of the church, James was poised for usefulness in ministry.

After the inauguration of the church on the Day of Pentecost, because the twelve apostles were frequently away preaching the gospel, James eventually became the preeminent leader of the church in Jerusalem. To borrow a contemporary term, he became its lead pastor.

James's ministry, along with the twelve apostles, was critical in setting the church on the right foundation. A major cornerstone in that regard came at the Jerusalem Council—where Peter, James, and the other apostles and elders clearly affirmed the gospel of grace as the true gospel (see Acts 15). In many ways, James was the first model pastor. Unlike the twelve apostles, who eventually left Jerusalem to take the gospel throughout the world,

James never left. He stayed with the church he loved, leading it faithfully for more than thirty years until the day he was killed.

Much of what we know about James's character and personality comes to us through the New Testament letter he penned. Even a quick read through the epistle of James reveals its strong emphasis on application—a trait that reflects the shepherding heart of its author. His letter stresses the application of truth, emphasizing the spiritual fruit that should characterize the life of every true Christian. Its tone is both personal and pastoral. James was a man who practiced what he preached, and who lovingly led that initial generation of believers in Jerusalem to do the same.

> James stayed with the church he loved, leading it faithfully for more than thirty years until the day he was killed.

The Lord created, called, saved, and equipped James for usefulness in manifesting His glory. He does the same for all believers (Romans 8:29). Like James, we were all filled with contempt and hatred toward God at one time. But if we have come to saving faith in Christ, we, too, have each been forgiven and equipped for spiritual service. Our salvation has been fully secured by grace through faith in Christ. Now, as James emphasized in his epistle, we must put feet to our faith—faithfully living in submissive obedience to the Word of God. In such living, our own story will unfold to the honor of the Lord Jesus, who is not ashamed to make us part of His family (cf. Romans 8:16–17).

How do we see God's grace to James despite a lifetime (until mature adulthood) of his rejecting the Messiah?

_____

_____

_____

Consider how far the Lord has brought you in Christ. List some of the fruit of His grace in your life that you never could have imagined possessing before your salvation.

_____

_____

_____

How have you been putting feet to your faith lately, as James so helpfully outlines in his epistle?

_____

_____

_____

Mark

Get Mark and bring him with you,
for he is useful to me for ministry.

2 TIMOTHY 4:11

In Acts 12, we read about Peter's miraculous escape from jail after an angel came and set him free. It was such a surreal experience that Peter didn't believe it was really happening. He thought he was simply seeing a vibrant vision—that is, until he found himself outside the prison walls on the streets of Jerusalem.

Coming to himself, he realized he may only have a few minutes until the guards noticed he was gone. So what did he do? Peter headed to the closest place of refuge, "the house of Mary, the mother of John whose surname was Mark" (v. 12).

This is the first mention of Mark in the New Testament, but it sheds a great deal of light on who he was. Apparently, Mark's mother was a devout Christian, and her house was a meeting place for the believers in Jerusalem. From this, we can know that Mark had undoubtedly been reared in the truth.

Around the time of Peter's release, Paul and Barnabas came to Jerusalem from Antioch in Syria with an offering from the believers there. Once their delivery was complete, as they prepared to return to the church they co-pastored in Antioch, Paul (still called "Saul") and Barnabas decided to bring an extra traveler back with them. As the biblical account explains, "Barnabas and Saul returned from Jerusalem when they had fulfilled their ministry, and they took with them John whose surname was Mark" (v. 25).

In Colossians 4:10, we learn that Mark was the cousin of Barnabas, which explains why he invited him to come to Antioch. Clearly, Barnabas must have trusted him, recognized his giftedness, and convinced Paul that he would be useful to their ministry among the Gentiles. Mark must have proved himself a valuable assistant because, when Paul and Barnabas left on their first missionary journey, they took Mark with them.

From the start, the ministry faced difficulty, and after a short while, the relentless struggles took the heart out of John Mark. Whatever the last straw, Acts 13:13 records the sad tale of his decision to abandon the mission: "Now when Paul and his party set sail from Paphos, they came to Perga in Pamphylia; and John, departing from them, returned to Jerusalem."

Evidently overwhelmed by the challenges and fearful of the outcome, Mark panicked and left, not for Antioch and the church he had been serving there, but straight back to his mother's home in Jerusalem.

> From the start, the ministry faced difficulty, and after a short while, the relentless struggles took the heart out of John Mark.

There was no excuse for Mark's cowardice—a fact that is confirmed in Acts 15. Several years had passed when Paul and Barnabas decided to embark on a second missionary journey (circa AD 50). "Barnabas wanted to take John, called Mark, along with them also. But Paul kept insisting that they should not take him along who had deserted them in Pamphylia and had not gone with them to the work" (vv. 37–38 NASB). The key word in that passage is *deserted*. As Paul reminded Barnabas, Mark was a deserter, a weak-hearted soldier who flees from the field of battle.

In the end, their disagreement over Mark caused a rift between Barnabas and Paul. Barnabas took Mark with him and headed to Cyprus, while Paul chose Silas and traveled through Syria and Seleucia.

After leaving with Barnabas in Acts 15:39, Mark disappeared from the annals of church history for the next decade. But that was not the end of his story. His name reemerges in a most unexpected place, roughly ten years later, when Paul, under house arrest in Rome, wrote a letter to the believers in Colossae. At the end of that epistle, he listed the names of those who were ministering to him during his imprisonment. Included in that list is none other than Mark. Paul included him along with others in a commending tribute.

A decade earlier, Paul had considered Mark an unreliable coward. Now he commended him to the Colossian believers as a man whose companionship brought comfort and joy to him in personal hardship. Years later, in what was likely Paul's final letter, he told Timothy, "Get Mark and bring him with you, for he is useful to me for ministry" (2 Timothy 4:11).

Mark's life is a wonderful example for anyone who's

ever given up when he was scared, who's ever quit for all the wrong reasons. It's never too late to change course and show oneself to be a reliable and devoted disciple of Jesus Christ.

How are you tempted to make excuses for your failures (youth, hardship, etc.)?

_____

_____

_____

How does Scripture encourage us with the record of John Mark's failings?

_____

_____

_____

What can we deduce is commendable about the decade in which Scripture tells us nothing of Mark's doings? How does this instruct you in how you should respond to your own failings?

_____

_____

_____

Onesimus

I appeal to you for my son
Onesimus, whom I have
begotten while in my chains.

PHILEMON 10

Onesimus was not a believer when he violated Roman
law and ran away from his master—Philemon, a
Christian man who lived in Colossae. It is safe to assume,
because Philemon was a believer and a leader in the
Colossian church, that he was a gracious and fair master
(cf. Philemon 5). But Onesimus wanted his freedom and
found an opportunity to snatch it.

Fleeing to Rome, he hoped to be lost among the
masses that thronged the imperial capital. But he could
not hide from the One who was seeking his soul. Though

the circumstances are not revealed to us in Scripture, God brought Onesimus to Paul—and to the gospel of freedom found in the Lord Jesus.

It is very likely Onesimus had heard Paul's name when he was still at his master's home in Colossae. The church met there, after all. Philemon may have even taken him to hear Paul preach when the apostle was in nearby Ephesus. Perhaps, after Onesimus came to Rome, the Spirit of God convicted him of his sin, and he sought out the apostle for help. Whatever the explanation for their meeting, one thing is clear: once Onesimus met Paul, his life was permanently changed because through Paul he met the Lord Jesus.

A runaway slave was a felon—guilty of a serious crime. Onesimus was a fugitive—a wanted man in the eyes of the Roman justice system. He had not only defrauded his master of his services but likely stolen goods or money from Philemon when he left (Philemon 18). Once he became a believer in Christ and was reconciled to God, Onesimus had no

> Once Onesimus became a believer in Christ and was reconciled to God, he had no choice but to go back to his master and be restored as his slave.

choice but to go back to his master and be restored as his slave.

The necessity of sending Onesimus back to Colossae became more urgent when Paul finished his epistle to the church in that city. Along with it, a second letter—a personal appeal from Paul to Philemon regarding the returning slave—was sent. According to Colossians 4:7–9, the apostle dispatched a man named Tychicus to deliver those letters, along with "Onesimus, a faithful and beloved brother, who is [now] one of you." Together, Tychicus and the fugitive slave headed for Colossae on their vital mission.

Because slaves were expensive and valuable, and because the Romans were always wary of the possibility of a slave uprising, they often dealt harshly with rebels and runaways. But Onesimus was willing to face his master and take that risk. Not only had he been radically transformed by Christ, he also knew the genuineness of his master's faith. Onesimus undoubtedly rested in the fact that both he and Philemon ultimately served the same Master. No matter what the outcome, the right thing to do was to seek Philemon's forgiveness.

The implication of Paul's letter to Philemon, supported by the testimony of church history, is that Philemon responded exactly as Paul expected he would.

According to ancient tradition, after they reconciled, Philemon sent Onesimus back to Paul, where he continued to serve and minister to the apostle.

Circa AD 110, an early Christian leader named Ignatius, the bishop of Antioch, wrote a letter to the church at Ephesus. In that letter, he addressed the bishop of Ephesus multiple times—repeatedly noting that the leader of the Ephesian church was a man named Onesimus! Could this be the same Onesimus as Philemon's runaway and reconciled slave? There are good reasons to think so. Paul's epistle to Philemon was written five decades before Ignatius's letter to the Ephesians. If Onesimus were a young man (in his early twenties) when Paul wrote (circa AD 61), he would have been in his early seventies when Ignatius penned his letter. That age would certainly be appropriate for a bishop in the early church. Some New Testament scholars have even suggested that Onesimus was likely instrumental in collecting and preserving the letters of Paul.

God is in the business of changing defectors from weak vessels into powerful agents of His revelation and salvation. For Onesimus, the forgiven fugitive, the story of his life points clearly to the One who rescued him, refusing to let him go even when he tried to run away. What joy there is for us as believers—to know that despite all our failings, we can never outrun God's grace or His plan to use us far beyond what we could ask or imagine.

Review some of the elements of Onesimus's life that make his conversion so remarkable. How do these show you the depth and strength of God's grace?

_____

_____

_____

Is your identity with Christ compelling you to make right some issue from your past? How can you do it with the courage and obedient conviction that Onesimus exemplified?

_____

_____

_____

How does the testimony of Onesimus's life help you worship the Lord better?

_____

_____

_____

Paul

*I determined not to know
anything among you except Jesus
Christ and Him crucified.*

1 CORINTHIANS 2:2

Well known and dreaded throughout the early church as
Saul of Tarsus, Paul was the most feared and ruthless per-
secutor of Christians, passionately "breathing threats and
murder against the disciples of the Lord" (Acts 9:1). Then
Christ stopped him in his tracks one day on the road to
Damascus, instantly transforming his heart and dramatically changing the whole course of his life (vv. 3–19).

Unlike the other apostles who had spent time with
Jesus during His earthly life, Paul received the gospel
directly from Christ by special revelation. He wrote to the

believers in Galatia, "I make known to you, brethren, that the gospel which was preached by me is not according to man. For I neither received it from man, nor was I taught it, but it came through the revelation of Jesus Christ" (Galatians 1:11–12). He was appointed by Christ to be an apostle as "one untimely born" (1 Corinthians 15:8 ESV).

Even though his conversion came after Christ's ascension, no one did more than Paul to spread the gospel across the face of the Roman Empire. Luke carefully chronicled Paul's three missionary journeys in the book of Acts. Beginning in Acts 13 through the end of that book, Paul becomes the central figure. And Luke's record of Paul's ministry is breathtaking. Paul's influence was profound wherever he set foot. He preached the gospel, planted churches, and aided new believers no matter where he went—from the land of Israel, throughout Asia Minor, across Greece, through Malta, Sicily, and finally to Rome. And while doing all that, Paul wrote more New Testament epistles than any other author. In an age long before modern

> The apostle Paul had an extraordinary gift for bringing the gospel message to light in just a few clear, well-chosen words.

conveniences made travel and communication relatively easy, Paul's accomplishments were extraordinary.

It is clear from the book of Acts and his letters that Paul felt a significant weight of responsibility to preach and defend the gospel. Wherever he went, agents of opposition to the gospel followed close behind, attacking the message he proclaimed. The powers of darkness seemed keenly aware of Paul's strategic role, and they focused their relentless attacks against the churches where his influence was especially strong. Therefore, Paul was constantly engaged in "the defense and confirmation of the gospel" (Philippians 1:7).

So much controversy surrounded Paul and his ministry that almost no one wanted to be identified with him. Had Paul not been a man of such profound faith, he might have died feeling alone and abandoned. As it is, he most likely did not fully realize how far his shadow would extend over the church and how deeply his influence would be felt by generation after generation of believers. But he did not die discouraged. He knew the truth of the gospel would ultimately triumph. He understood that the gates of hell would never prevail against the church Christ is building. He remained confident that God's purposes would assuredly be fulfilled—and that God's plan was indeed already being fulfilled, even as he anticipated his own impending martyrdom. He wrote, "I am already being poured out as a drink offering, and the time of my departure is at hand. I have fought the good fight, I have finished the race, I have kept the faith. Finally, there is laid up for me the crown of right-eousness, which the Lord, the righteous Judge, will give to me on that Day, and not to me only but also to all who have loved His appearing" (2 Timothy 4:6–8).

The apostle Paul had an extraordinary gift for bringing the gospel message to light in just a few clear, well-chosen words. His epistles are filled with brilliant, one-verse summaries of the gospel. Each of these key texts is different from the others. Each has a distinctive emphasis that highlights some essential aspect of the good news. Any one of them can stand alone as a power-ful declaration of gospel truth. Or put them all together, and you have the framework for a full-orbed understand-ing of the biblical doctrine of salvation.

Though Paul occupies a unique role in the history of redemption not to be repeated, there is much to emulate in his devotion to Jesus Christ: his passion to reach the lost with the gospel, his willingness to suffer for Christ, and his brilliant exposition of the Scriptures. Above all,

Paul was obedient to the Savior he loved, willing to do whatever and go wherever the Lord commanded.

How did God choose to save the apostle Paul? In what ways does Paul's conversion parallel your own salvation?

_____

_____

_____

Consider all Paul was able to accomplish for the gospel's spread, even before modern conveniences existed to aid him in that. How are you using the means God has given you to extend the gospel's reach?

_____

_____

_____

What guarded Paul from discouragement? How are you applying the same attitude in your life?

_____

_____

_____

The Prodigal Son

And the son said to him, "Father,
I have sinned against heaven and
in your sight, and am no longer
worthy to be called your son."

LUKE 15:21

The parable of the prodigal son is perhaps the greatest short story ever told. The character of the younger son—the Prodigal—has much to teach us about our plight as sinners and the unfathomable grace of God.

When we are first introduced to the younger son in Jesus' parable, the picture painted is that of a young man, probably in his teens and obviously filled with shameless disrespect for his father. For a son in that culture to request his inheritance early was tantamount to saying,

"Dad, I wish you were dead. You are in the way of my plans. I want my freedom. And I want out of this family now. I have other plans that don't involve you, this family, or this estate. I want nothing to do with any of you. Give me my inheritance now, and I am out of here."

Faced with such a request, any self-respecting father in that culture would have felt he had to disgrace the son as publicly as possible. After all, it was the only way to avoid allowing the boy to bring a lasting reproach against the family's good name. Instead, the father in this parable "divided to them his livelihood" (Luke 15:12).

It didn't take long for the real agenda behind the Prodigal's defiance to become clear: "And not many days after, the younger son gathered all together, journeyed to a far country, and there wasted his possessions with prodigal living" (v. 13). When the Prodigal arrived in the far country, he was a fat cat with a big bankroll. You can bet every con artist and lowlife in town set their sights on him. But whatever "friends" the Prodigal made in the pursuit of such a lifestyle were no true friends at all. When he ran out of cash, they were nowhere to be found.

Right after the Prodigal spent himself broke, "there arose a severe famine in that land" (v. 14). Here was an absolutely devastating turn of events. Consider how hard it must have hit the Prodigal. His father had met his every need and supplied him with every amenity from the day he was born. Now not only had the life of pleasure he sought come to a screeching halt, but also it was suddenly clear to him that the life of freedom he thought he would find was nothing like he anticipated.

Before long, the Prodigal found himself feeding swine—virtually the lowest and most possibly degrading chore in the whole hierarchy of labor. As he watched the pigs greedily devouring the carob pods he gave them, he found himself earnestly longing to fill his own stomach with the swine food. It was at this low point that he finally came to his senses and decided to return to his father's home, not as a son—he had behaved too wretchedly for that—but as a servant.

As he drew near, the Prodigal must have rehearsed his plea dozens, maybe hundreds, of times: "Father, I have sinned against heaven and before you, and I am no longer worthy to be called your son. Make me like one of your hired servants" (vv. 18–19). But as he drew closer to his family's estate, he saw something in the distance—his own father, running toward him.

We can safely imagine that the father had been looking steadily, scanning the horizon daily, repeatedly, for signs of the boy's return. How else could he have seen him while he was still a long way off? When the father spied his beloved lost son, he gathered up the hem of his robe and took off in a most undignified manner, truly eager to initiate forgiveness and reconciliation. The father clearly wanted to reach the Prodigal before the boy reached the village—apparently to protect him from the outpouring of scorn and criticism he would surely have received if he walked through that village unreconciled with his father. The father himself would bear the shame and take the abuse instead.

This is indeed a fitting picture of Christ, who humbled Himself to seek and to save the lost—and then "endured the cross, despising the shame" (Hebrews 12:2). Like this father, He willingly took upon Himself all the bitter scorn, the contempt, the mockery, and the wrath our sin fully deserves. He even took our guilt upon His own innocent shoulders. He bore everything for our sake and in our stead.

> When the father spied his beloved lost son, he gathered up the hem of his robe and took off in a most undignified manner, truly eager to initiate forgiveness and reconciliation.

What parallels do you see between your own attitudes and those of the prodigal son at the parable's beginning?

_____

_____

_____

Reexamine the son's planned speech upon returning home. Does your heart reflect the same estimation of your standing before God? Why or why not?

_____

_____

_____

What does Jesus' characterization of the father in His parable tell you about God's disposition toward undeserving sinners?

_____

_____

_____

The Elder Brother

But he was angry and would not go in.

LUKE 15:28

The Prodigal is emblematic of the brazen rebel, straight-forward in his evildoing, not caring who sees what he does. Faced with the reality of his own fallenness, this sinner is more likely to repent and seek salvation. His sin has already been uncovered and is therefore undeniable. He *has* to face up to it. The Prodigal's elder brother, however, was a sinner of the secretive, hypocritical variety, not unlike the Pharisees to whom Jesus first addressed this parable.

The elder brother's most obvious characteristic is his resentment for his younger brother. But underneath that, and even more ominously, he clearly has been nurturing a quietly smoldering hatred for the father—for a long, long time, it appears. This secretly rebellious spirit has shaped and molded his character in a most disturbing way.

People often assume that the elder son represents a true believer, faithful all his life but suddenly caught off guard by his father's generosity to the wayward brother and therefore a little bit resentful. That interpretation misses the whole point of the parable, though. The elder son has never truly been devoted to his father. He is by no means symbolic of the true believer. Instead, he depicts the religious hypocrite.

The elder brother probably had the whole village sincerely believing that he was the "good" son—very respectful and faithful to his father. He stuck around the house. He pretended to be a loyal son. However, he had no genuine respect for his father, no interest in what pleased his father, no love for the father's values, and no concern for his needy younger brother.

The Prodigal Son's brother had been out in the field that day, unaware of the celebration that was already underway at his house, even though the whole rest of the village had been in a buzz about it for hours. It was late in the evening, perhaps even dark already, when the elder brother showed up. Here was the biggest event the village had ever seen—the greatest celebration his family had ever hosted—and he knew nothing about it.

It is a striking fact that neither the father nor anyone else had told the elder son about his brother's return. There's only one reasonable explanation. This son had no better relationship with his father than the Prodigal did when he first left home. The father surely knew that—even if no one else did.

The elder son must have known very well how much his father loved the younger brother. Anyone could easily see what an ache the father had carried in his heart every single day since the Prodigal ran away. If the stay-at-home son had truly loved his dad, whatever made the father rejoice should have been an occasion for him to rejoice as well. But the elder brother did not respond that way. He remained outside and demanded to know what was going on before he would even think of joining the festivities.

Moments later, the father arrived on the scene. Fed up and angry, the elder son tore the veil off his own hypocrisy and unloaded his bitterness: "Look! For so many years I have been serving you and I have never neglected a command of yours; and yet you have never given me a young goat, so that I might celebrate with my friends; but when this son of yours came, who has devoured your wealth with prostitutes, you killed the fattened calf for him" (Luke 15:29–30 NASB).

Grace is the only hope for any sinner. But the elder brother didn't see himself as a sinner in need of grace. The truth is, however, that he needed the father's forgiveness and mercy as much as the Prodigal did. Instead of resenting the father's kindness to his brother, this son should have been the most eager participant in the celebration because he, too, was in desperate need of that kind of mercy. If he had simply had an honest understanding of the wickedness of his own heart, he would have seized on the father's mercy as the greatest reason of all to rejoice.

> If the elder brother had simply had an honest understanding of the wickedness of his own heart, he would have seized on the father's mercy as the greatest reason of all to rejoice.

The invitation to be part of the great celebratory banquet is open to all. If you are still alienated from God, Christ urges you to acknowledge your guilt, admit your own spiritual poverty, embrace your heavenly Father, and be reconciled to Him (2 Corinthians 5:20).

What does the Scripture text tell us is the elder son's nature and personality?

_____

_____

_____

Explain why Jesus' narrative does not support that the elder son is merely a true believer caught off guard by his father's generosity.

_____

_____

_____

Identify how the elder son's grasp of truth was deficient. What about his grasp of love? What parallels to his faulty perspectives do you see prevalent in the world today?

_____

_____

_____

Jesus

And the Word became flesh and dwelt
among us, and we beheld His glory,
the glory as of the only begotten of the
Father, full of grace and truth.

JOHN 1:14

In the final verse of John's gospel, the beloved disciple declares, "There are also many other things that Jesus did, which if they were written one by one, I suppose that even the world itself could not contain the books that would be written" (John 21:25). If John was so constrained, there is no hope that a chapter such as this could adequately summarize Jesus Christ. Yet it would hardly do to choose forty lives from the pages of Scripture and ignore the one life that gave life to all others.

At the center of God's plan of redemption is Jesus. He is the author and perfecter of our faith (Hebrews 12:2), the Savior of our souls (Luke 2:11). He is the Alpha and the Omega, the first and the last (Revelation 22:13). He is the Word made flesh (John 1:14), the one and only Son of God, and the hope of the world (3:16). He is the Messiah (4:25–26), the Lamb of God (1:29), and the Lion of Judah (Revelation 5:5).

Perhaps the most common descriptor for Jesus is "Lord." He is called Lord (*kurios* in the Greek text) no fewer than 747 times in the New Testament. The book of Acts alone refers to Him as Lord 92 times, while calling Him Savior only twice. Clearly in the early church's preaching, the lordship of Christ was the heart of the Christian message.

To say that Jesus is Lord is first to acknowledge that He is almighty God, the Creator and Sustainer of all things (Colossians 1:16–17). This is a profound declaration of truth. There is little question that the Bible teaches that Jesus is God; only cultists and unbelievers dispute this truth. In John 10:30, He said plainly, "I and My Father are one." Jesus' critics clearly understood He was claiming to be God on this (v. 33) and many other occasions (e.g., John 5:18; 8:58–59; Mark 14:61–64).

We are seeing God in action when we read of the works of Christ. When we hear His words as recorded in the New Testament, we are hearing the words of God. When we hear Christ express emotion, we are listening to the heart of God. And when He gives a directive, it is the commandment of God. There is nothing He does not know, nothing He cannot do, and no way He can fail. Jesus is God in the fullest possible sense.

As God, Jesus is the sovereign Lord, and the influence of His authority extends to every person. In fact, all judgment has been committed to Him: "For the Father judges no one, but has committed all judgment to the Son" (John 5:22). Notice the reason for this: "that all should honor the Son just as they honor the Father" (v. 23). Likewise, those who dishonor the Son by rejecting His right to be sovereign also dishonor the Father. In the final judgment, every knee will bow and every tongue will confess Christ as Lord, to the glory of God the Father (Philippians 2:11–12).

> Jesus surrendered the glories of heaven to become one of us and willingly die the most painful, humiliating death known to mankind.

Although He is sovereign God, Jesus took upon Himself the limitations of human flesh and dwelt personally among sinful men and women (John 1:14). While on earth, He experienced all the sorrows and tribulations of humanity—except that He never sinned (Hebrews 4:15). He surrendered the glories of heaven to become one of us and willingly die the most painful, humiliating death known to any human. He did it on our behalf. Though He was sinless, and therefore not worthy of death (cf. Romans 6:23), He suffered the guilt of *our* sin: "He Himself bore our sins in His body on the cross, that we might die to sin and live to righteousness" (1 Peter 2:24 NASB).

Jesus said, "Come to Me, all you who labor and are heavy laden, and I will give you rest" (Matthew 11:28). The invitation is open to all, and Scripture assures us that salvation belongs to those who receive Him (John 1:12). Yet none of us can come on our own terms; we must receive Him for all that He is—"The blessed and only Sovereign, the King of kings and Lord of lords" (1 Timothy 6:15 NASB).

Explain what it means to identify Jesus as Lord.

_____

_____

_____

Give examples of how Jesus is the fullness of God's expression.

_____

_____

_____

How do you know you have responded to Christ's invitation to receive salvation?

_____

_____

_____

Steps to Peace With God

1. God's Purpose: Peace and Life

God loves you and wants you to experience peace and life—abundant and eternal.

The Bible says ...

"We have peace with God through our Lord Jesus Christ." *Romans 5:1, NKJV*

"For God so loved the world that He gave His only begotten Son, that whoever believes in Him should not perish but have everlasting life." *John 3:16, NKJV*

"I have come that they may have life, and that they may have it more abundantly." *John 10:10, NKJV*

Since God planned for us to have peace and the abundant life right now, why are most people not having this experience?

2. Our Problem: Separation From God

God created us in His own image to have an abundant life. He did not make us as robots to automatically love and obey Him, but gave us a will and a freedom of choice.

We chose to disobey God and go our own willful way. We still make this choice today. This results in separation from God.

The Bible says ...

"For all have sinned and fall short of the glory of God." *Romans 3:23, NKJV*

"For the wages of sin is death, but the gift of God is eternal life in Christ Jesus our Lord." *Romans 6:23, NKJV*

Our choice results in separation from God.

Our Attempts

Through the ages, individuals have tried in many ways to bridge this gap ... without success ...

The Bible says ...

"There is a way that seems right to a man, but its end is the way of death."
Proverbs 14:12, NKJV

"But your iniquities have separated you from your God; and your sins have hidden His face from you, so that He will not hear."
Isaiah 59:2, NKJV

There is only one remedy for this problem of separation.

3. God's Remedy: The Cross

Jesus Christ is the only answer to this problem. He died on the cross and rose from the grave, paying the penalty for our sin and bridging the gap between God and people.

The Bible says ...

"For there is one God and one Mediator between God and men, the Man Christ Jesus."
1 Timothy 2:5, NKJV

"For Christ also suffered once for sins, the just for the unjust, that He might bring us to God."
1 Peter 3:18, NKJV

"But God shows his love for us in that while we were still sinners, Christ died for us." *Romans 5:8, ESV*

God has provided the only way ... we must make the choice ...

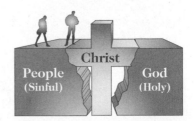

4. Our Response: Receive Christ

We must trust Jesus Christ and receive Him by personal invitation.

The Bible says ...

"Behold, I stand at the door and knock. If anyone hears My voice and opens the door, I will come in to him and dine with him, and he with Me." *Revelation 3:20, NKJV*

"But to all who did receive him, who believed in his name, he gave the right to become children of God." *John 1:12, ESV*

"If you confess with your mouth that Jesus is Lord and believe in your heart that God raised him from the dead, you will be saved." *Romans 10:9, ESV*

Are you here ... or here?

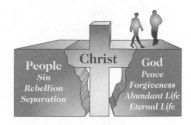

Is there any good reason why you cannot receive Jesus Christ right now?

How to Receive Christ:

1. Admit your need (say, "I am a sinner").
2. Be willing to turn from your sins (repent) and ask for God's forgiveness.
3. Believe that Jesus Christ died for you on the cross and rose from the grave.
4. Through prayer, invite Jesus Christ to come in and control your life through the Holy Spirit (receive Jesus as Lord and Savior).

What to Pray:

Dear God,
    I know that I am a sinner. I want to turn from my sins, and I ask for Your forgiveness. I believe that Jesus Christ is Your Son. I believe He died for my sins and that You raised Him to life. I want Him to come into my heart and to take control of my life. I want to trust Jesus as my Savior and follow Him as my Lord from this day forward.

                    In Jesus' Name, amen.

_____   _____
Date   Signature

GOD'S ASSURANCE: HIS WORD

IF YOU PRAYED THIS PRAYER,

THE BIBLE SAYS ...

"For 'everyone who calls on the name of the Lord will be saved.'"
Romans 10:13, ESV

Did you sincerely ask Jesus Christ to come into your life?
Where is He right now? What has He given you?

"For by grace you have been saved through faith. And this is not your
own doing; it is the gift of God, not a result of works, so that no one may
boast." *Ephesians 2:8–9, ESV*

THE BIBLE SAYS ...

"He who has the Son has life; he who does not have the Son of God does
not have life. These things I have written to you who believe in the name of
the Son of God, that you may know that you have eternal life, and that you
may continue to believe in the name of the Son of God."
1 John 5:12–13, NKJV

Receiving Christ, we are born into God's family through the
supernatural work of the Holy Spirit, who indwells every believer.
This is called regeneration or the "new birth."

This is just the beginning of a wonderful new life in Christ. To deepen
this relationship you should:

1. Read your Bible every day to know Christ better.
2. Talk to God in prayer every day.
3. Tell others about Christ.
4. Worship, fellowship, and serve with other Christians in a church where
   Christ is preached.
5. As Christ's representative in a needy world, demonstrate your new life by
   your love and concern for others.

God bless you as you do.

Franklin Graham

If you want further help in the decision you have made, write to:
Billy Graham Evangelistic Association
1 Billy Graham Parkway, Charlotte, NC 28201-0001

1-877-2GRAHAM (1-877-247-2426)
BillyGraham.org/commitment